Praise for *Loveable*

From Single Women:

"For the first time, I'm meeting men who embody my wish list, honor me, support me, respect me and are in awe of me. It's a must read for anyone seeking a loving and healthy relationship!" – Jill

"I was able to let go of a relationship that surfaced its ugly head before it got started again." – Christina

"When reading the book, it was scary how much I could relate so much to so many of your dating stories and how you used to tick! I've always wanted to say, 'I love this and that and the other thing,' but tried to find less passionate words for things I, um, love. But no more!" – Sarah

"I love the title: *Loveable*. It's so perfect, just beautiful, one simple word. That is what we all need to strive for! Today I went to the athletic club with a new feeling about myself. I looked at the men differently, with a twinkle in my eye and my head tilted to the side, in a playful manner. It felt good, free. When I was at the pool, I talked with a woman friend and she was into her negative talk about men. I encouraged her to tell the guys she's dating that they weren't the right matches for her, in a way that honored herself and them! Hey, I learned it!" – Joy

From Single Moms:

"My favorite chapters provided concepts that I had never considered before: *Love Languages, Communication Must-Haves with Men,* and *Now, Not Later.* Someone who is single and looking for a relationship should buy this book if they want to end up in the relationship they want. Knowing what you want is the first hurdle. I immediately took action after completing the Lightening the Load exercise. I discovered through this practice the power of letting go of the past. I could see what was coming up in each of my romantic relationships and with men in general." – Asha

From Women in Healthy Relationships:

"If you're tired of trying your best at relationships only to keep being disappointed, YOU NEED THIS BOOK. It's chock full of insightful tips and practical actions you can take that will make a difference in how you experience relationships." – Alice

"It was great to see you and I love your book. Solid and useful information delivered in a charming and easily digestible style." – Andrea

From Married Women:

"Even if you are married like I am (almost 47 years), this book helps you find your power again. You realize you had an identity before marriage and children. This book gives you the freedom to be you in a loveable way!" – Arlene

"I really enjoyed *Loveable* and took much of the coaching to heart. It's so easy to become complacent in a marriage and forget to make your partner feel loved and appreciated. I am asking for his help nicely again and remembering to thank him in a way that makes him feel like a hero. Thank you so much for improving my husband's life!" – Sherilyn

"I am really impressed with Suzanne's book, *Loveable.* Not only will Suzanne's advice help me in my relationship of 28 years but also in my professional life. It's *my* job to make *me* happy instead of pushing the responsibility over to my partner. Communication: It's important how to communicate with my partner and the people around me. I shouldn't criticize. I can't expect my partner to read my mind. Be candid and straightforward in expressing my needs but not without a sprinkle of sweetness. Forgiveness is an important part of having a good relationship; not only forgiving my partner but also myself for past mistakes." – Ruth

11/26/18

Loveable

Suzanne Muller-Heinz

Loveable

21 Practices for Being in a Loving & Fulfilling Relationship

By

Suzanne Muller

EXPRESSIONIST
DENVER
COLORADO

Loveable

Published by Expressionist Press LLC
Denver, Colorado
www.expressionistpress.com
877-926-9300

ISBN 978-0-9851631-4-3

Dedication

To my parents, John and Arlene Muller, for giving me life, loving me and allowing me to learn the hard way at times. It is because of you that I have grown to be the person I am today.

To my boyfriend, Stefan Heinz, who loves me for who I am and has our relationship be tender, fun, fulfilling and playful. You are truly my playmate and teammate, and I love sharing life with you.

Table of Contents

About the Author

Ugly, loser, scared, unworthy. These are all words I've used to describe myself over the last forty years. I've also called myself needy, weird, clingy, naïve, confused and single forever. Over the last ten years, I've been engaged twice and never married. I've also been hurt, heartbroken, stood up, and cheated on. I've been broken up with via text and voice mail, yelled at, stalked, and on the delivery end of a few broken hearts. In the process, I've been swept off my feet, gone to wonderful places, dated multiple people at the same time, and dated online. You name it, and I've probably been through it!

After considerable self-reflection, I decided to embark on a journey that changed my life forever. I became a "student" of men, women, love, dating, healthy relationships, and myself. I sought out and used many resources on this trip of self-discovery. Some of my academic and non-academic learning experiences included a Communications Minor at San

Jose State University, Landmark Worldwide (Communication Courses, Wisdom Unlimited Course, Leadership Program and Direct Access), Access Consciousness, and The School of Hard Knocks.

Today, I'm deeply connected to my heart, gifts and divine feminine energy. I live with my amazing boyfriend Stefan in Switzerland, one of the most beautiful countries in the world, and I feel like the luckiest woman alive.

We met in Cancun, Mexico. Our first date was swimming with dolphins. We said, "I love you," on the fourth day we knew each other and "yes" to being in a healthy relationship together on the fifth day. We dated long distance between Denver, Colorado and Freienbach, Switzerland for eight months.

Our relationship is a partnership in every sense of the word—love, trust, honor, happiness, ease, generosity, support, joy, laughter, fun, simplicity, lightness, adventure, and authentic communication are all present. Now that we live together, we travel for fun about twice a month. Most days, except when Stefan travels for business, we work from home and enjoy quality time together.

I finally found my playmate and teammate. I must say, every tear, every bad date, every dollar spent on self-improvement, every minute waiting for a guy to call or ask me out was time, money and energy well spent. I realize it was all part of my process and journey.

Now, as a worldwide Dating and Love Life Coach, Speaker and Author, I regularly work with clients in Colorado, New York, Washington State, Kansas, Ireland, Canada, Germany, and more. My passion in life is to help single people around the world discover happy, healthy relationships and fall in love with great partners.

For over nine months, I provided the Happy Living Forever segment as a weekly correspondent/guest on the Boomer and Women's Radio Network, a division of Clear Channel Communications. I reached an audience of more than 50,000 around the world as a guest on The Jerry Bovino Show. I've also been a radio show guest on Advanced Living, Naked Radio, and Temptation Time with Tiffany. My teaching at Colorado Free University was exciting as I taught students new techniques for success with their online dating profiles.

A few years ago, I invented my purpose in life. It's been my mantra and what strengthens my heart every day. It reminds me who I am, and why I'm here on this planet. My purpose is to use my unique gifts in communication and listening to empower all people so that they know their greatness. My dream is to expand the world's capacity to listen and speak from LOVE and to create a world filled with effective communication, love, and peace.

This book is a compilation of the successful practices I used, so that you can take some shortcuts to the beautiful, tender and fulfilling relationship you desire and deserve. I truly hope my practices assist you in your journey to a fun dating life, a fulfilling relationship, and love.

Foreword

"Welcome to the adventure of a lifetime!"

I offer my clients this bold greeting as they begin their book-writing journey—and I am not kidding in any way, shape or form. As any published author will tell you, it is an adventure. I often compare the process of writing a book to running a marathon. It sounds like a good idea, until you actually wake up at five a.m. on a frigid morning and strap your shoes on already blistering feet and it dawns on you that perhaps you are in way over your head. Thus, the starting line is full of new authors raring to go—and the finish line is sprinkled with the glorious few that are brave enough to have completed the race. The true champions are those who have gone the distance so that others can benefit from their wise words.

Thankfully for those still searching for love, Suzanne Muller is one such champion, and *Loveable: 21 Practices for Being in a Loving & Fulfilling Relation-*

ship is a first-prize winner. Suzanne was willing to go the distance in her commitment so that you, dear reader, could have the love that you crave.

Here is what it takes to succeed as an author: You must have a vision worth sharing and a passion that goes the distance. You must be willing to stare at a blank page for hours upon hours, battling gremlins of self-doubt as fragmented thoughts swirl through your head while you seek to express your heart-felt message. Then, you must rally to market your fledgling idea and seek a publisher. These are all daunting tasks even for the boldest of us. Add in that all along the way, authors face seemingly endless criticism and rejection. It's no wonder that out of the 80% of people that say they want to write a book, only a mere 4% actually will complete this momentous task.

Suzanne never gave up on herself as an author—and she never gave up in her stand that all who seek will find long-lasting love. She never quit writing when the going got tough, when the inspiration faded, when she grew tired of sitting day after day in front of the blank page waiting for the muse to appear. Because of Suzanne's ceaseless commitment, you now have the valuable wisdom contained in this book.

Drawing on her vast knowledge as an International Dating and Love Life Coach, her experience as a radio show correspondent, as well as her own insightful (and heart-wrenching) forays into the dating world before finding true love, Suzanne Muller is the expert to turn to for *anyone* seeking love. As you progress through this book, you will be embarking on your own adventure. You can relax into Suzanne's savvy and hard-earned guidance. Through illuminating practices, you will discover a plethora of opportunities to master this crazy thing called love. You will uncover hidden traps that interfere with you living and loving powerfully.

With honesty and humility, Suzanne lets you know you are not taking this journey alone. She has been there and she bravely shares her ups and downs along the perilous path of finding love. The only difference is, with Suzanne as your guide, the path is no longer frightening. Instead, it is one of the greatest journeys you will ever take.

You won't be preached to, scolded or made wrong. You will be loved, supported and encouraged—until you are ready to jump off the sidelines and into the great ocean of love that is waiting for you.

In the 21 practices contained in *Loveable,* one practice builds upon the next to prepare the ground for love. Some of what you will discover on your way to relationship success is to truly leave behind any dating mishaps and heartbreak—bouncing forward into a more joyous you. You will finally figure out what *you* really want in a relationship versus endlessly trying to be what you think others want. In one of my personal favorites, you will learn how to fix your "busted man-picker" and find relationship freedom!

Your goal in picking up this book may be to find love—and if you follow these practices you cannot fail in that. Even more importantly, you will start living the life you have always wanted. As with any true champion, Suzanne will never let you down. *Loveable* is no Band-Aid® approach to dating and love. Nor will you simply find partnership. Instead, you will create lasting happiness within a relationship. You will learn to love yourself and discover just how fabulous you are, and then you will learn how to receive love.

While it's not an easy process, it will be one of the most rewarding things you ever do—in fact it can be a state-changing, life-altering, and mind-blowing experience!

The best part is, as you prepare for the relationship of your dreams, you will discover the most fabulous person on earth is standing *right now* in your shoes. That's right, it's you!

Again, I welcome you to the adventure of a lifetime!

Welcome to *Loveable*!

Kristen Moeller, MS
Bestselling author of *Waiting for Jack* and
What Are You Waiting For: How to Rise to the Occasion of Your Life
Executive Publisher, Imbue Press

Introduction

"Success comes from preparation."

– E'yen A. Gardner

The dating world has changed, and falling in love seems to be harder than ever. Most people in the dating pool are just trying to survive and keep their heads above water. You may be someone who doesn't even want to jump in. I understand, believe me. Before I met my wonderful boyfriend Stefan, I went through the tsunami of the dating world. I was caught in a sea of poor choices, stuck in the swirl of relationships that ended with abandoning ship after about five weeks, treading water, and feeling resigned, alone and frustrated. I would always jump in again, though.

That's what we do. Because we want what's on the other side: being in love with a great partner.

Facing upset, annoyance and frustration over and over again, I was just about to throw my hands up and say, "Forget it." Then, after considerable reflection, I decided to embark on a journey that changed my life forever.

I began to develop the muscle to consistently follow my heart, trust my instincts, honor myself and find a path to real happiness. I'll be teaching you how to do the same throughout this book. Today, I'm deeply connected to my internal and external beauty, my gifts and my heart. I own my power and divine feminine energy. You, too, will gain this knowledge by doing the practices in this book.

Most of us have experienced a dissatisfying or unhealthy relationship we'd rather forget. You may have some heartache lingering from your past or a hurt still lurking that makes you hesitant to meet someone or to trust a man. The last thing you want is one of *those* relationships again. You will have a chance to clear out some of that leftover baggage in the pages ahead.

I often share my own experiences of failure and frustration, as well as successes and joys. I reveal my disappointments and triumphs. As a dating and love coach, I give you the scoop on all that I learned and discovered so you don't have to learn the hard way. I want you to have a fulfilling, loving and healthy relationship, and I will help you get there.

Forty-three percent of all Americans over the age of 18 are single, according to the U.S. Census Bureau. Of those single people, 61% have never said, "I do." Twenty-four percent are divorced and 15% are widowed. In the European Union (EU), 17.5% of all households are single adults (stats are for those under age 65). One-person adult households are expected to increase to 36% by 2015, according to Demographic Research magazine, August 2011. The statistics worldwide, if readily available, would likely be very similar. The good news is that 43% of people are single. With 7 billion people on the planet, there have to be a lot of good men out there.

My point is that if you think all the good ones are taken, then think again. Great men are out there, I'm here to tell you. It may be that the old way you are approaching dating just isn't working. When you have read this book and done all the practices, you will be able to believe it is possible for you. It's time to go in the water again and be successful.

After dating for many years, I sometimes thought being alone would be a much easier route to go—until I found a fulfilling relationship that blew the doors off everything I ever thought was possible. I can now adamantly profess it is worth the journey, worth the reflection, and worth learning the skills. Those skills are outlined in the practices in this book just for you. I only dated Stefan for four days before we knew we wanted to be in a committed relationship, and on the fifth day we jumped in. Though this isn't typical, it is possible, especially when your own heart is ready and you are feeling *Loveable*.

This book is not so much about do's and don'ts as it is about you getting back in touch with the concept of being *loveable*. Most of all, I want you to know to your bones that you can fully love a man, that he can completely love you, and that you will love and honor yourself, first and foremost.

Our human tendency is to want connection. We yearn for that special person and relationship, the one that really works. As humans, we are meant to be interconnected. With our ever-growing, busy lives, we may have to adjust the way we think and how we select a "healthy" person for us. We need to be smarter about who we spend our time with, invest our emotional energy in, and give our heart to. If we didn't believe the end result would be worth all the time, emotional energy and money, most of us would choose to be single and alone—and settle for watching others from our safe, poolside lounge chairs.

When I finally learned how to make dating work for me and how to love and honor myself, everything changed. My true love appeared in my life easily and quickly. I also became more comfortable with letting someone really love me, and I learned how to fully love someone else.

The practices ahead are the things I did to become loveable, allow love in, and love and honor myself. I am giving you many exercises and practices that I learned along the way. Had I known them earlier, I would have saved many years of dating on and off, massive amounts of energy, buckets of tears, and countless bad dates. I call them practices because they are habits to acquire, with steps to perform and exercises to work through to acquire skill and proficiency. They worked for me, and I'm excited to hand them to you to help you be successful. I hope to provide you with some shortcuts to prevent you from experiencing the same constant swirl of dating or the fear of putting your toe in the water that I experienced.

This book is designed to assist you in eliminating unhelpful feelings about meeting someone and help you transform dating into one of the best experiences of your life. In the pages ahead, I'll show you how dating can flow beautifully into an amazing relationship if you are willing to make the effort and do the work. If you like things simple and easy, like I do, I can promise you the possibility of someone walking right into your life. Let's make this journey simple and fun.

Included in this book are ways to:

- Heal the hurt from past relationships and move forward with ease, clarity and confidence.
- Maximize your time, emotional energy and money.
- Enjoy the dating process.
- Align your thoughts and wants with what will actually fulfill you as a woman.
- Stay focused on the end result—a healthy and fulfilling relationship.
- Learn to trust yourself and men again. Be open, yet smart, and allow love to walk into your life with ease and simplicity.
- Attract someone healthy and great for you.
- Become someone who can maintain and sustain a healthy relationship once you discover it.
- Be loved by a man and love him completely while loving and honoring yourself.

We will explore how to increase your confidence exponentially, so you are clear and confident that you *are* a great partner inside and out. What if you truly had the confidence and skills to know your days of being single were numbered? What if you knew there was a line of men waiting in the wings for you because you are that great?

These tools are meant to prepare you, your heart, and your emotions to meet someone to share your life with. You'll enjoy a greater sense of fun, ease, confidence and freedom in the process. If you follow these practices and make them habits, you will be able to jump out of singlehood and into a fulfilling relationship. Most of all, the level of love you experience all around you will be extraordinary. The pages that follow blend smarts, intuition, heart and good choices with caution and trust.

You are busy and your time is precious, which is why I put together this new approach. This is not a "how to date" book, although it will give you lots of ideas about how to meet someone, how to interact better with a man, and, most of all, how to be a woman men want to be in a partnership with.

New Definitions for a New Dating World

At this point, let's consider some new definitions that could bring more clarity to terms that tend to frighten people away. I'm not looking to update *Webster's Dictionary*; rather, I want to show you a new way to define a few key terms based on your goal of redefining relationships for yourself.

Traditional definitions for *dating, relationship* and *partner* feel very outdated, unappealing and boring. I think it's time we recognize how much the world has shifted. We can demand that our own personal life be a reflection of something that's rewarding, fun and fulfilling. Let's give new meaning and freshness to these words. Below, you'll find my version of these words for the kind of relationships single people yearn for.

Dating: An opportunity to get to know someone as a *possible* partner. A means toward the healthy relationship you desire. A step toward a lasting relationship. A fundamental way for single adults to go out with new people, go to fun places, and discuss topics that are important to them to determine if they are compatible with each other. Dating is the action you take to meet someone: an action that forwards the personal goals, desires and dreams of being in a romantic relationship while having fun and connecting with different people.

Healthy Relationship: A fun, light, simple and easy way of being with someone. A connection that makes life easier, happier and more fulfilling. A partnership that works for both people, where communication is authentic, honest, and a two-way street. Both people are heard, and it becomes easy to work through issues together. It's full of connection, intimacy and romance. Real relationship includes two people who respect, appreciate, adore and honor one another. In addition, a healthy relationship is one where you have individual goals as well as goals as a couple, to forward your life and your dreams. It's fulfilling, healthy and growing every day with more love, gratitude and trust.

Partner: Someone you can share life with: a playmate and a teammate. A partner has your back and is your biggest champion. It is someone who is dependable, reliable, and that you can count on to have fun, push you to be your best, and trust completely.

After reading these definitions, wouldn't you agree they are more appealing to pursue than some older definition you had? Now, let's discuss how you can experience them for yourself!

The practices in the chapters ahead are designed to help you heal past hurts and open your heart to experience a love you've only imagined—or maybe never dared to imagine for yourself. They will empower you to discover your own ability to love a man *and* yourself better than ever before. They will guide you to experience yourself as loveable.

How Best To Use this Book

This book is your guide to having the most fulfilling relationship of your life. It provides exercises, questions and practices to increase your confidence and appreciate your own worth and value. You'll gain knowledge about men and create what your ideal relationship will be. The best part is that you will be well prepared to welcome the love of your life with open arms and an open heart. If you are serious about discovering an awesome partner, creating a loving and fulfilling relationship, and having it last, then join me in exploring these 21 practices that will help you be successful. This book can be used alone, or you can grab a single friend and do the exercises together.

By doing these exercises and keeping these practices in motion in your life, you will never lose yourself in a relationship again. You'll become a love magnet. You may be wildly surprised how much more attractive you become to men.

The Starting Point

Jumping into the dating world head first without knowledge and preparation can be a recipe for struggle, hurt and hard work. Who needs that? You need a starting point to determine how ready and available for love you really are.

For example, if you've been running casually for several years, and your new goal is to run a marathon, would you continue the same actions? No, you'd assess your running style and then learn the best ways to accomplish your goal to run that marathon successfully. Likewise, if you love to cook, and you've recently decided to become a chef for a living, would you continue to only cook for yourself? Probably not. You'd test your current cooking skills and learn where you need to go from there to become a chef that high-class restaurants would want to hire.

After many surveys, a lot of research and countless discussions with clients, I have found that it's easier and smoother to meet someone, date, and embrace love with a healthy partner when you have developed skills and abilities in some key areas. Understanding your starting point is a very important part of the process. It can also be the most difficult because it's the most revealing. If you are not ready for the emotional rollercoaster of dating, you can get caught up in a dysfunctional past pattern or perhaps be attracted to a relationship that doesn't serve you.

I'm a firm believer in the phrase "knowledge is power." The following survey will give you knowledge of where you are now, and it will reveal where you'll need to grow to have the relationship you want. When you understand the areas in which you are strong and the ones in which you are weak, you can be more aware of what you need to focus on to be successful. That's the good news. You now have a point of reference, and you will see movement and progress as you work through the rest of the practices and exercises in this book.

When answering the questions below, be honest and truthful with yourself. Remember, it's just the starting point.

On a scale from 1 (low) to 10 (high), rate yourself on the following:

1) How much do you trust men? 5
2) How comfortable are you in the dating process? 5
3) How beautiful do you think you are? 8
4) What is your ability to have a healthy relationship that could last a lifetime? 8

5) How confident are you that you can have a man who adores, cherishes, loves and even worships you in a healthy way?

6) How much do you love and honor yourself?

7) Where would you rate your ability to accept and receive love from a man expressed in emotional, physical and financial ways?

8) How much do you trust yourself?

9) How would you rate your communication skills for maintaining and sustaining a healthy relationship?

10) How would you rate yourself as a great date?

11) What is your ability to make men feel great about themselves?

12) In life right now in general, what is your level of happiness and fulfillment as a person?

Congratulations on completing the assessment. Take a minute to look at your answers again. The numbers don't mean anything about you as a person. Instead, they represent your current pulse on the status of your skills and situation in the dating world. There is nothing wrong or right about them; there's just the honest truth about where you are right now. The questions, practices and exercises to follow in this book are designed to raise all of your numbers to eights, nines and tens. I also recommend retaking this survey after you have read the book, completed the exercises, and put the practices into full practice in your life for several months. In my research, most of the women in healthy relationships were at nines and tens, so these numbers are achievable. You can do this!

My client Brenda is a good example of someone who made progress quickly and easily.

> *"I can't believe how much has shifted for me in three months of dating coaching. I have not yet met the man I will share my life with but I know he is out there and that together we can be happy and fulfilled. My feelings on meeting and dating men and finding my life partner have changed from fear, inadequacy and resignation to excitement, hope, anticipation and even a touch of impatience! Now that I know who I am searching for, the dating process is a matter of the quality of connections I can make rather than the quantity of attention or acceptance I receive. My fears of rejection have lessened greatly. I am now looking for someone I can be happy with instead of hoping that all the men I meet will like me. By going through the exercises and doing the homework, I have let go of regrets and self-criticism, and my self-confidence has improved immeasurably. I am really looking forward to meeting my future partner. In the meantime, I am having fun talking to strangers and being the real me in all company."*

Now that you have a clear picture of your starting point, it's time to create a new destiny and step into it.

Practice

Your New Destiny

"Love is our true destiny. We do not find the meaning of life by ourselves alone—we find it with another."

—Thomas Merton

In this first practice, we start unraveling some feelings and attitudes that are often in the way of finding lasting love. Every relationship we have provides us with something—some good things and some things we would rather forget. We have a tendency to carry the bad stuff with us to the next relationship to be sure we don't do *that* again. As we date or interact with men, there are things that have built up over the years that we may or may not even be aware of. A lot of people call this baggage or junk. I'm going to call it "leftovers." Here are a few examples:

- You've just been dumped, or your guy broke up with you out of the blue. Your leftover is, "Guys dump me out of the blue."
- You were seeing someone you thought was really great, but it turns out he was lying to you. Your leftover might be, "Men lie," or, "If he seems great, then he's going to lie."
- He stopped calling with no communication or warning. You're getting the idea; you fill in the blank.

When situations like these happen, the leftovers get stuck in our hearts, minds and souls. If they stay there unresolved, they can make surrendering to love the next time it comes along even more challenging.

A few years ago, I was in an exclusive dating relationship—or so I thought. One day, as I was sitting in a business meeting, I received an email from someone I didn't know. The email said that the man I was dating had been her boyfriend for the last year. She had also copied several other women on the email after hacking into his computer to inform all of us of his actions and behavior. I was devastated and shocked when I learned the man I had been dating was cheating on me. Things like that didn't happen to me. Not only was he cheating on me, but he was doing so with at least four other women. When he confirmed all this, the news rocked me to my core.

Do you think I felt like going openly and freely back into the dating scene and trusting men again after that? No. I said to myself, "Men are untrustworthy. Men are cheaters. Men are unsafe. I don't know how to select a good man for me."

When crummy feelings build up inside, no matter how small they are, it can become more difficult for you to draw a healthy partner into your life. The leftovers you're carrying around will bring up some version of fear, frustration and worry. These emotions are not conducive to a healthy relationship. Where does love fit in there? It would be a tight squeeze.

Many years ago, a friend introduced me to the following exercise. I now use it for my clients and myself. I've found it to be very effective in the arena of dating, men, healthy relationships, and love.

After being cheated on and dating men that weren't good for me, I would sit down and do this particular exercise. I knew in some way I was still thinking too small when it came to the type of man I needed to be with and the kind of relationship that was possible. This exercise alone inspired me, gave me freedom, and allowed me to envision a new future that I could live into. It will help you to think outside the box, wish big, dream to the stars, *and* have that dream come true, if you are willing to put forth the effort.

Before you create your new destiny, I want to share some additional inspiration. My friend Shannon took my first-ever workshop, held on my backyard patio several years ago.

> *"Before taking Suzanne's workshop, I longed for a relationship, yet didn't believe it could really happen. I was a single mom with a full-time job and many commitments. I felt that being in a relationship would jeopardize my daughter's happiness and well-being. In past relationships, I got engrossed in the newness of it all and let important commitments fall by the wayside. I couldn't afford to let that happen with my daughter in the picture. Clearly, it was safer to just put off romance until she was grown. For nearly 11 years I harbored resentment toward other couples as I suppressed sharing love and intimacy.*
>
> *After taking Suzanne's workshop, I had a clean slate and I created the possibility of just connecting with someone. If it led to a relationship, great; if not, great. The important part was I created how I was going to be for myself, for a possible love interest, and for my daughter. I gave myself a new outlook on love! Now I'm in a relationship that has continued to grow and blos-*

som for over two years. I continue to use the techniques I learned from Suzanne on how to grow my relationship and steer it in directions that inspire my boyfriend, my daughter and me. I am truly grateful that I am free to express myself fully in this area of my life."

I recommend looking at this exercise as a fun way to allow yourself to tell the truth. Please be incredibly honest because what's on the other side of it is the best dating life and the healthiest relationship you've ever dreamed of and never in a million years thought you could be in.

Are you ready? Let's clear out your leftovers!

1. Please grab a notebook, journal, loose paper, steno pad, iPad or computer and jot down the following phrases. I recommend about four lines in between each. There are many exercises coming throughout the book, so I would recommend having this handy as you go.

    - **Dating is…**
    - **Men are…**
    - **A relationship is…**
    - **Love is…**

    Take several minutes and write all of the words, phrases and thoughts that pop into your mind about these particular areas. For example, you might write, "Dating is…fun, hard, exhausting, scary," or "Men are…strong, confusing, unavailable, sexy," and so on. You get the point. There are no right or wrong adjectives to use, so don't hold back. Write every word or phrase you can think of or that's right there at the tip of your tongue. The more honest you can be, the better.

2. Look at what you have written. Ask yourself if your life in these areas resembles those words? As the next step, cross out any of the words or phrases that don't serve you anymore, carry negative connotations, or you just don't like. Go ahead and cross them off. As you are crossing off the words, say or think, "Goodbye."

   Keep crossing off words until the only ones left on the paper are the words you want to keep or that seem inspiring and empowering to you. Good job! What did you notice after crossing out the negative words on your page? What words are left?

3. For this next part, turn the paper over or grab a clean sheet of paper. Write down these phrases with about four lines in between each phrase:

   - **Dating is…**
   - **My man is…**
   - **A healthy relationship is…**
   - **Love is…**

This is your opportunity to invent your new destiny from scratch in these areas.

A Couple of Suggestions:

- If you still love some of the words you wrote down in the first phase of the exercise, transfer them over to your new destiny.
- Try not to look backwards. See if you can look into your future. Consider that you are working on a blank canvas and write new, fresh words and thoughts.
- Start writing your new destiny and think as big as you can.

  Take the next few minutes to write motivating words, phrases and thoughts for each area. Take your time, as this is your new destiny for dating, men, a healthy relationship and love. Think of this exercise as *fun* and exciting. After you are done writing these new words, phrases and sentences, take a minute to reread each area.

Congratulations for thinking big and writing your redesigned destiny! Feel free to toss the original out. Take another minute to consider: Does this new destiny bring a smile to your face? If this destiny came true, would you be happier and more fulfilled? Even if only 90% came true, would that be a great relationship and destiny to have? If your answer is no, redo the exercise.

Looking at your new destiny, ask yourself if you are willing to have it come true. At this moment, you may have a little, "Yeah, right," going on. That's okay. After this exercise, most people are usually a little resigned, but some people say, "Yes, of course, that's the destiny I've always wanted." Either way is great. You may never have thought this big, and it may not seem possible right now. This is normal because as human beings, we tend to think a bit small. You've done the exercise right if:

- This new destiny is more inspiring than that first one you wrote.
- You feel lighter by looking at this new destiny, even if you are a bit resigned or cautious.
- You would love to have this new destiny come true versus the first one you wrote.
- You can see what's possible now, even if you don't believe it quite yet.

Over the next several days and weeks, read your new destiny over and over. I recommend you keep it somewhere accessible to you and read it every couple of days. It is one thing to write a new destiny. Now the work begins: feel it, think it, and believe it. Over time, the resignation will lift and you will start to feel it *is* possible. If you can write it and want it, then you can have it!

Some Suggestions:

- Post your new destiny somewhere you can easily see it, like the computer monitor, bathroom mirror, closet door, or the refrigerator.
- Read it often and allow yourself to feel what it will be like when it comes true.
- From now on, when you are out dating and meeting men, let this be your guide and pulse. Ask yourself, "Does this experience look and feel like my new destiny?" If not, this man may not be the partner for you. If it feels good and aligns with your new destiny, then he could be someone to keep dating and exploring with. It is that easy.

This is a great step toward having your newly invented destiny become real for you. Your next challenge is to keep resignation or pessimism from creeping in. Believe me, it will try. If you are out there dating, meeting men and your new destiny is not here yet or does not quite feel like what you want, then repeat the exercise. My relationship and fantastic boyfriend are most of what I wrote down in my future destiny, and more. I had to do it three times before I could think big enough for him to finally show up, so hang in there. It might take just once for you. That would be terrific!

Now that *you* have a future destiny to look forward to, this next practice is going to plunge you into a new layer of leftovers and will provide a new level of love.

Practice #2

Lighten The Load

"Freedom is what you do with what's been done to you."

—Jean-Paul Sartre

After inventing a new destiny, we're going to dive into something a bit deeper, yet very important. During your life thus far, have you been in a relationship you would rather forget or are still trying to forget? Perhaps it feels like it is haunting your mind. Have you been in a relationship that left you resentful about what happened? Have you ever stayed too long in a relationship when you knew in your heart you should have left sooner? Believe me, most of us have.

This practice will release more of those unhealthy relationship "leftovers" from your mind, body and heart. This allows more room for an amazing man and a healthy relationship to show up in your life. It will lighten your load and give you tremendous freedom from past relationships. Let's begin!

1. Think about a previous relationship with a man you still think about from time to time. Think about the person who still nags at you based on how the relationship went, how he treated you, or how it ended. If you still have some negative feelings or regrets toward him, you are on the right track. Yes, that man. Some of you may have one, two, or more of these. Don't worry; you are not alone. Make sure you do this exercise for *each* relationship about which you have hurt feelings or regrets.

Next, take out your dedicated notebook and answer the following questions. This may take between 15 and 30 minutes, depending on how much you have to write. Give yourself ample time. Start with the person who *most* tugs at your heartstrings.

- What do you want to say about the relationship you had with this person? How did the relationship go? Be sure to keep writing until your mind is emptied out.

- What do you want to say to this person? (Imagine this person is standing right in front of you with tape over his mouth so all he can do is listen.) This is your opportunity to say exactly what you need to say because either you didn't get heard when you were with him, or you may have been afraid to communicate while you were with him. Give it everything you've got. This is your opportunity to write it in your own words and express it in your own way. Don't hold anything back.
- What regrets do you have about being with that person? What regrets do you still have about the relationship? List all of them no matter how big or small.

2. Now, take a few deep breaths. Bring tons of love, compassion and generosity to your body, mind, heart and soul. Breathe deeply again, and ask yourself this question: Am I willing to forgive him for all of this? See if you can bring forgiveness into your whole body and forgive from your heart. Don't force it, but know that forgiving will set *you* free. If you are struggling to forgive, take another deep breath and see if you can forgive this person as a human, as a

young boy who didn't have good relationship skills, or better yet, who was being an idiot.

3. Most of the time, forgiving someone else is the easier part. Let's shift toward you. Can you forgive yourself for:
    - Being with someone who treated you this way?
    - Staying with the person as long as you did?
    - Allowing yourself to be taken advantage of and/or dishonored?
    - Letting yourself be verbally or physically abused, if you were?
    - Making a poor choice?
    - Not standing up for yourself?
    - Anything else you can forgive yourself for?

Focus on your breath as you forgive him for each of these areas. Keep breathing and let the forgiveness flow into your cells, your blood, your heart, your soul. Let the energy flow from your toes all the way up to your head. If it makes a difference, close your eyes. See how much generosity, love and compassion you can let permeate into your body.

When you have forgiven him and yourself, speak the words, "I forgive you for all of it." Now, take a deep breath, and continue writing out the following answers.

4. What did you learn about relationships by being in this relationship? What did you learn from this person? What did you learn about yourself?
5. You were with this man because you found some good qualities in him. What can you thank this person for? If you have written it all out and written everything there was to write, you should see at least a couple of things.
6. Is there anything else that you would like to communicate to this person or about the relationship? Finally, write any last thoughts that you'd like to communicate to this person about this relationship.

Congratulations! That's a big step in releasing your leftovers and the stuff that's been blocking your heart.

At this point, you may feel a little tired or exhausted. You may feel lighter, you might be sad, or you could be experiencing more freedom. Whatever you are feeling at this time is perfect. Allow yourself to feel your current emotions. You just released a lot in this exercise.

Having written all there was to write, this is a wonderful time to discard what you wrote. Tear up the paper or hit the delete button. Trust me, it's very therapeutic to eliminate all that and send it to the garbage. As you do, say, "Thank you and goodbye." You can even wave it goodbye if you'd like. This is also a great time to make a pact with yourself, like a pinky swear, that you will never be with someone like that again! Draw the line in the sand and make a promise to yourself. Keep the good qualities you saw in that person and toss the rest.

Congratulations for making the time and doing the work! Over the next few days, you may have thoughts of this person because this exercise can stir things up. As the thoughts come up, just say, "Thank you." You'll be surprised how easily those thoughts fade. Soon the good memories of this person will prevail.

If you've had several past relationships that linger with you, I recommend going through this practice as many times as you need to in order to fully benefit from forgiving each person and yourself. If you have, or had, a poor relationship with a parent, I would recommend going through this same exercise. You'd be surprised how much something that happened with a parent can leave you stuck with men. The more you release, forgive and forget, the healthier your mind and heart will be. You're preparing to welcome in a bigger and better relationship. In the process, you'll set yourself up for a loving, fulfilling and satisfying future. After doing this work for myself with all of my ex-boyfriends and even people I felt resentful toward, I can now focus my attention on my current romantic relationship, and have it be the best it can be. It's magnificent.

These last two practices were the tough ones. It may have felt like you were going through the eye of a needle. Congratulations for doing this work! Give yourself some applause!

After releasing and letting go of your leftovers, you are now ready for the next few practices, which will focus you on filling yourself up with love. You'll also learn how to avoid letting so much negativity accumulate again. That's the good news. Great job! Now, there is more work for us to do.

Practice #3

Flood Yourself with *Love*

"For one human being to love another; that is perhaps the most difficult of all our tasks, the ultimate, the last test and proof, the work for which all other work is but preparation."

—Rainer Maria Rilke

After engaging in the last two practices, you could be feeling like a weight has been lifted from your shoulders. You still might be a little tired. You've taken a big step. Bravo! This next practice will help you see the amount of love you award yourself on a daily basis and give you simple ways to improve it. It's also a great way to fill back up with love after releasing a lot of emotion in the previous exercises.

As a society, we are starving for love and often go looking for it from other people first. This is a pitfall that I have fallen into in the past. I had to learn over time not to do that. This practice will show you how you can raise your level of love for yourself almost instantly, resulting in a new ability to receive a healthy kind of love from a partner.

Consider the following questions: How much do you *flood* yourself with love on a daily basis? What if you could increase the amount of love you experience every day with a few simple steps?

If you were to rate the portion of love you actually grant yourself on a daily basis, what grade would you currently give *yourself*? Would you give yourself an A (Excellent), B (Above Average), C (Average), D (Below Average), or F (Poor)? Keep in mind that any grade you start with is a great starting point! Most of us think we love ourselves a lot. However, the harsh reality is that we don't.

When I finally realized how much I'd given over to others the responsibility of making me feel loved instead of replenishing myself, I was appalled. I was surprised I had not yet shriveled up from a lack of self-love.

For example, I noticed how frequently I would answer an email quickly because I didn't want someone to get mad at me. I often picked up the phone even when I wasn't in the mood to talk. I jumped to help someone when I didn't have enough time. Sometimes I agreed to do something for someone even though I was exhausted and running on fumes. My "to do" list was huge, and it was running my life. Every fifteen minutes seemed to be scheduled with more things to do. My guilt often outweighed the love I had for myself. I saw how unworkable my life was in that state. Was I trying to be overly busy to mask how unloved I felt? Perhaps.

I believe that in a romantic partnership between a man and a woman, the woman is an essential, nurturing source of love. If you are running on fumes or even on empty, are you able to give whole-heartedly to the relationship? I highly recommend shifting this behavior by strengthening your muscle to stop, look, consider, and then act.

A client recently told me she goes to work, runs to the gym, takes a quick shower, and then goes on a date two to three times a week, literally rushing from place to place. What she saw was that she needed to slow down and not do so many things on the same night so she could enjoy each of them more. She even started spending some nights at home alone to have time to think, thus honoring herself and enjoying downtime. She still had a lot of friends and a busy social life; however, she also feels more peaceful and in tune with her thoughts and feelings.

Most people are pulled by their surroundings, busy environments and to-do lists. Women are awful at using the word "*no.*" Everyone is tugging at us and, most of the time, we succumb. There is such an impact on our lives in terms of our time, energy and heart. By staying this busy and not honoring ourselves, we can become resentful, feeling empty, unfulfilled and drained. This leaves us with little love to give out. I bet we have all said or heard a girlfriend say, "I *lose* myself when I'm in a relationship." Our inability to say "no" is a major reason why this happens!

Drenching yourself with love also means not being afraid to take the time to think, consider, and then act. When you pause to consider all of your options and proceed with the one that truly honors you, the feeling of satisfaction can arise. The stronger this muscle becomes, the simpler life can be. Making decisions and choices becomes easier. Believe me, when you are in a healthy relationship, this practice will provide you with love for yourself, love for your life, and love for your man. If you continue doing this exercise regularly, the man you are with will know you are a woman who thinks before she acts—and that's *sexy*!

In this activity, identify actions you take where you do not honor or love yourself.

1. Over the next couple weeks, notice how often you:
   - Act out of guilt.
   - Put yourself on the back burner for someone else.
   - Go against your own heart and instincts.
   - Say "yes" when you mean to say "no".
   - Do something when you really didn't want to.

   Take as much time as you need to look at your own daily life. Once you've identified how often you do these things, you're going to start catching yourself at them. Now, you'll have the opportunity to do things differently or to stop doing them altogether.

2. Taking time for yourself is part of honoring and loving the *you* of you. Over the week ahead, take an occasional moment to **stop**, **think**, **consider,** and **act** on the question, "If I follow my heart, trust my instincts and honor myself, what would I do in this moment?" You're likely

to start saying "*no*" more often and feeling loved as a result—by you.

Remember, all of this is practice. You're building the muscle to be in a relationship where your needs are met so you will have a lot more love to dish out. As you flood yourself with love, you'll also open yourself up to *receive* the kind of love your heart desires from a man. Later in the book, we'll talk about pampering and being spoiled.

Practice #4

A Secret to Happiness

"There is only one happiness in this life, to love and be loved."

—George Sand

Happiness is a common topic of discussion lately, understandably so. I hear time and again from clients who are unhappy about how often they have given too much of themselves in one-sided relationships. It's one of the biggest reasons many women are hesitant to jump into a new relationship. I don't blame you one bit if you are one of them. I was. I didn't want to keep repeating that cycle, either. The good news is it can be different.

If you have given away a lot of your time and energy over the years, you're probably fairly exhausted. You may even wonder if relationships can be a two-way street. This practice will help you start to shift that concern. Why bother? Because being exhausted, tired and resentful doesn't make you happy, does it? No! However, it's human to feel these emotions. Let's look to see how you can change these emotions quickly and easily back into happiness.

Have you heard the saying, "When Mama ain't happy, ain't nobody happy?" The problem is our society has a tendency to think the man is supposed to make the woman happy. That's nonsense. Maybe this belief is left over from a previous generation; I don't know for sure. Let's put this concept to rest. Things have changed over time, and we need to adapt. I believe men can make you happ*ier*, but it's *your* job to make *you* happy. There is great power in nourishing yourself. That power allows you to be more loving, supportive, warm, sweet, happy and wonderful.

When I'm happy, I'm very sure that I'm happy, and others can see it. Would you agree that when you are happy, you feel it to your bones? Oddly enough, the biggest secret to master in order to attain happiness is identifying when you are *not* happy. The faster you build the muscle of identifying when you are *not* happy and knowing what would make you happy, the happier you will become. Here's why: When you can see you are not happy, then you have more choices.

This is where men come in. Men are great at fixing things. Naturally, if you're unhappy, the man you are seeing will want to do something to make you happy. That's the good news. However, your responsibility is to communicate very specifically what would make you happy. The key is to be honest, and that takes being highly in tune with yourself. One of my clients told me her boyfriend once said to her, "I think your 'wanter' is broken." He wanted to make her happy, but she was unable to tap into what it was she wanted or needed. Had she been more in tune with herself, she could have given him an honest answer, and he would have been thrilled to fulfill it for her.

Here is a pitfall that you want to avoid. You cannot tell a man half of what will make you happy. You cannot be vague about what will make you happy. You have to be clear and direct, yet kind. Can you see why it's important?

To help you grasp this concept, consider the following:

1. Stop, look inside, and ask, "What would make me happy?" Notice if anything comes up that sounds like, "I don't need anything," or "I don't deserve to have what I want." If that happens, look again. We all have needs, and we all deserve to have everything we're willing to receive.
2. If a man asks what you want, respond with the truth. Give him the real answer. Men love to see women tickled pink and blissed out. They feel defeated if they give you what you said you wanted and it still doesn't make you happy. Being sure of what you want and being straightforward about it can save you a lot of time, grief and unnecessary arguments. We can't expect men to read our minds. Men do better when women are up-front, open and honest.
3. Sometimes you may not care about being happy. You may just need to be sad or tired. We all have those moments. If you know deep down he has no chance of making you happy in that moment, then again, it's your job to express yourself. For example, say, "I'm feeling sad right now and just want some time to myself." Or, "I'm exhausted and just want a nap." Once you communicate what you need to him and he honors your request, it becomes your assignment to take the action and bring yourself back into the happy state again. If you

> request a nap and then say, "On second thought, I'm not going to take a nap, I'd rather go to the store with you," you'll confuse him. If you waver in your communication, can you see how the action could be confusing to him? It also demonstrates to a man that you don't honor yourself, and he could start to lose respect for you.

When my client began to practice giving straightforward and honest answers to her boyfriend, it felt awkward to her at first and seemed a bit selfish. After several attempts, she started to see how much her man wanted to make her happy. It became natural for her to recognize and ask for what she really needed. At that point, their relationship began to change from being one-sided to being a beautiful give-and-take partnership.

When you open yourself up to asking for and receiving that which makes you happy, you won't find yourself in one-sided relationships ever again. It does take some practice, and you can do it!

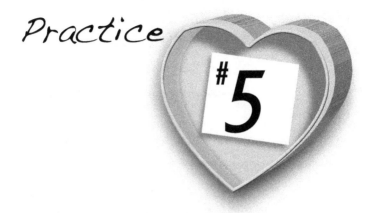

Practice #5

Love Languages

"Where there is love there is life."

–Mahatma Ghandi

Do you know your love language? Do you know his? The love languages described in *The 5 Love Languages,* by Gary Chapman, are critical to landing the love of your life and keeping it alive and fulfilling. Please read this section with new eyes, whether you've heard of these five love languages before or not. If you haven't read the book, I highly recommend doing so. This information can save you a lot of time and heartache. This chapter will provide you with a summary of this valuable book. I'll also give you some helpful practices to start understanding your own love language as well as that of your potential partner.

I can't stress enough how important the love languages are to finding the love you want and nourishing the love you find. They assist in uncovering what fills your love cup to the brim and unveiling what your partner desires. Determining each other's love languages early in your relationship is critical to learning about each other's needs.

First, let's touch on why having a good grasp of the love languages is essential for keeping *your* cup full to overflowing. When your love cup isn't overflowing, what could happen? You might become annoyed, irritated, depressed, worried, scared, grumpy, or unhappy. Does any of this sound familiar? Who wants to be around you when you are feeling this way? You may even want to jump out of your own skin and run away from the situation when these moods set in. We've all been there. Having a new viewpoint on the love languages can decrease the frequency of these emotional surges, thus making you a more consistent and loving partner.

Although there are five love languages, I recommend you determine your *two* key love languages—the top one and the runner-up. Read through this list and see what stands out to you.

1. Gifts – you like to give and receive gifts.
2. Words of Affirmation – you like giving people acknowledgement and words of praise, and you feel loved when you receive them.
3. Acts of Service – you like doing nice things for people, and you feel loved when somebody does something for you.
4. Physical Touch – you like to touch people and be touched.
5. Quality Time – you crave time with the people you love, and you like the time to be meaningful.

Let me give you an example. My front-runner love language is Quality Time. It's the main way I connect with someone. For me, knowing when I will spend time with someone or when I will speak to them satisfies my heart. I don't mind if the time I spend with someone is fifteen minutes, three hours, or a full day, as long as that time is good quality time. It could include going for coffee at a café, a walk in the park, a good conversation, a dinner together at a restaurant, or a leisurely stroll in the mall. Quality time for me also can be watching a movie in silence, as long as we are together.

When I was dating, I felt ignored when someone I had spent time with didn't set plans for another date. It wasn't necessarily true that I *was* being neglected, but that's how it felt. I would then wait for the phone to ring, hoping he would communicate about a next date. This process annoyed me and often left me distracted and resentful. If the call didn't happen within two to three days of our first date, I would be short with him when he eventually did call.

When Stefan and I were dating long-distance, we were very specific about when we would Skype, talk on the phone, or see each other in person again. We made sure we had trips planned to see one another, which put my mind at ease. More importantly, not only did we discuss and plan Skype dates, we also added them to our calendars. Because of this small and simple action, I had peace of mind and did not find myself distracted during my day or wondering every evening if he was going to call. I was able to focus on the other things that mattered to me.

Now that we live together, we are still very specific about things. It's been this way from the onset, and it makes a world of difference for me in terms of feeling loved. It isn't that I'm nuts or a control freak, which is what I used to think. This kind of conscious awareness of *myself* and my need for quality time provides me with a new world of freedom and peace of mind.

My second love language is Physical Touch. Without touch I would probably shrivel up and die. It's *that* important to me, and it's taken me a long time to recognize that. I thought I was just needy and clingy, and now I realize it is part of the fulfillment and love that I require. Touch makes my heart clock tick. I love that Stefan is affectionate and welcomes my ways of expressing love through physical touch.

The key is being curious about which love languages you and your partner like to receive and which ones you like to *give*. People tend to give what they like to get instead of asking what the other person wants to get. Unless you and your partner know each other's love languages, neither of you will feel fulfilled. This is a big reason to discuss the love languages as early in the relationship as you feel comfortable.

How Do You Receive More Love?

Find a partner who enjoys filling you up with your love languages and vice versa:

1. Discuss the love languages with your date and future partner early on.

2. Differentiate which love language you like to give and which one you like to receive. Talk to your romantic partner and ask what his primary love language is. Perhaps the two of you can read the book together.
3. Talk about ways to use your love languages to build a stronger relationship.

When we express what we *like*, it's possible to receive more of it. Isn't that what being filled up with love, happiness and fulfillment is all about? We get more of something that feels good or even *great*. Shared knowledge is power in receiving what you want! When you have a great partner who loves you, he will want to know how to keep your love cup filled and overflowing.

Practice

Transform Your Thoughts for Success

"Once you replace negative thoughts with positive ones, you'll start having positive results."

—Willie Nelson

Our thoughts are stronger than we can imagine. Let's be honest, our normal day-to-day thoughts are dark and mean to us most of the time. Have you noticed that your thoughts are often not very efficient when it comes to altering your energy and fulfilling on your deepest desires and dreams? According to scientists who study the brain, its function is to keep you safe. To do this, it employs thoughts of worry and fear. However, those thoughts will *not* get you what you want and can keep you from a healthy and fulfilling relationship. Why?

Your brain will do its best to keep you safe in relationships. It doesn't want you to be rejected. "What?" you might ask. "My *brain* doesn't want me to get hurt? My *brain* doesn't want me to feel bad?" Yes, your brain. Your brain will give you signals of caution and concern. Sometimes, those thoughts can be important to listen to and take to heart. In this chapter we will discern the good thoughts, like your instincts or issues to discuss, as well as the thoughts that keep you away from your dreams.

Your brain would rather you be safe than vulnerable, so it will play tricks on you to keep you from putting yourself in a compromising situation. For example, when I was considering moving to Switzerland to live with Stefan, my brain did everything possible to prevent me from moving from my great, comfortable life in Denver. My brain conjured up thoughts like, "*It will not work out. I am being stupid. I can't do this. I'm not an international person.*" We all know that relationships are filled with risk and uncertainty, which can be scary. They can also bring joy, bliss and amazement to your heart. To your brain, it's dangerous to fall in love and let somebody in. That is why I'm going to distinguish between listening to the mind and listening to the heart. It's a fine line, but worth understanding.

Shifting your thoughts requires that you develop another muscle for your success now and in the future. In fact, it likely will be the thing that saves you while preparing for your partner, meeting different people and, more than ever, when you get into a fulfilling relationship. I wish I could say this is an easy one. I will say it is one well worth practicing over and over and over if you want to be successful in having a loving and fulfilling relationship. I know you want that.

A client who is dating someone new said to me in our coaching appointment, "Suzanne, I wake up every day and have to pinch myself and say, '*This is too good to be true. It's unbelievable how this feels.*'" Because she is almost mesmerized, her brain is trying to tell her the relationship is not real. She is already worried she will sabotage the situation. It's very scary for her because it feels so good.

I answered, "What if your love life really can feel that way most of the time? Are you willing to have that because you have done the work on yourself?"

She responded with a resounding, "Heck, yes!"

You do have to transform your thoughts. Otherwise, you might as well not waste your time dating because you're just going to do the same old thing. It's like Einstein's definition of insanity, but instead of doing the same things over and over and expecting a different result, you're thinking the same old things and expecting a different result. It is useless to continue doing it. We can transform that!

The next exercise includes steps and ideas about how to change your thoughts on your own. Your assignment will be to keep these new positive thoughts someplace where you can catch a glimpse of them until you believe them in your heart of hearts. The challenge we face is the deep resignation we silly human beings have about dating, relationships, love, and even life, sometimes. A new way of thinking might be uncomfortable for a few days until the thoughts become like walking. Trust me, what is on the other side is a new life of bliss and miracles. Consider it more productive to stay in the dating and relationship boat than to jump out at one glimpse of rocky waters.

Here's how this worked for me. I used to be a serial dater. My dating life looked like a never-ending revolving door of men. This always made me feel unwanted and hopeless. I knew something had to change, but I didn't know what. As you can imagine, my dating life felt like a pile of rocks that grew larger every day. It felt heavy; like I was almost suffocating, buried under something I couldn't escape. My friends were always asking me, "Who are you dating?" I was a five-week girl. I couldn't hold on to a man for more than five weeks without the relationship crumbling into dust. My life seemed like one date after another with me breaking up with the guy after one or two dates or the man disappearing into thin air. This pattern frustrated me. It also validated my pathetic stories of not being good enough and men always leaving me. Becoming more and more embarrassed, I even stopped talking about it.

I thought men were the problem. At least, I thought it was easier to point my finger at them. It wasn't. After pointing the finger back at myself, I finally changed my thoughts. My disempowering thoughts were: "No one wants me. He will leave me. I'm not good enough. I'm a loser." These thoughts nagged at me constantly. They did not seem like beliefs; they felt etched in stone and as real as the moon.

The method I used to transform my thoughts came from transforming other areas of my life. I was willing to see if focusing my attention on what I want rather than just hoping for it would work to transform this area of my life. Bound and determined, I started to think, "I'm going to meet my true love." In fact, I wrote TRUE LOVE in big letters on a small white board that hung on my refrigerator door.

One night I had a date over for dinner. As we sat at the table in my kitchen, the gentleman glanced up at the white board.

"What are those words about?" he asked.

I replied without any hesitation, "That's what I want." I was very adamant about it. I didn't hold back, and I couldn't have cared less about his judgment. I shrugged it off and went about flipping over my salmon to serve for dinner. Although he was a nice gentleman, it was our first and last date.

Every day I saw the words "True Love" beaming at me. There were days I walked away from it, bummed out and wondering if I was fooling myself. Interestingly, after a few weeks, I could feel my body sensations, my speaking, my actions, and my beliefs aligning with my desire: "I will meet my true love." How? When? I had no idea. I just believed and surrendered. To what? To God? Miracles? The Universe? My word to myself? Perhaps it was a combination of all of them.

It was like my cells and molecules were rearranging to align with my new thought. I didn't know when it would happen. I am now a firm believer that focusing on a specific outcome over time will train the brain to recognize opportunities to achieve it. When you see many new opportunities, it is easier to take actions consistent with achieving the result you want. Taking the right action when an opportunity occurs can make your dreams and desires reality. The practices in this book help you tune into the possibility of having a fulfilling relationship and be ready to take the actions to achieve it.

Now, the teamwork and partnership I experience with my boyfriend feels like true love from the ease, joy and flow of it. When people try to convince me you can't have everything you want and relationships are hard, I share my story. I also share my clients' successes, which they achieved because I helped them alter their thoughts. By transforming my thoughts, I invented my relationship from scratch, and you can too. Here are the steps:

1. Identify your self-critical or disempowering thoughts. One way to find them is to think about having a happy, healthy and fulfilling relationship that could last a lifetime. What's the first disempowering thought that pops into your mind? It might be something like: "Men never choose me;" "He will leave me;" "I don't

know how to have a healthy relationship;" "I'm too old;" or "I will screw it up."

2. Create a thought that's empowering and positive. Some examples could be: "I'm great at relationships;" "I'm with a man who adores me and I adore him;" "There are a lot of great men available and the right one will find me;" or "I'm surrounded by men who think I'm amazing and attractive." The key is to have a thought that makes you feel good.
3. Make sure your thought is big enough for what you truly desire.
4. Write or post the positive thought somewhere you will see it every day, perhaps in several places.
5. When you look at your new thought, soak it in and feel what it will feel like when it becomes real.
6. Feel the new thought in your body, mind and heart.
7. Watch for opportunities to take actions that will fulfill on your new thought and take those actions when you can.
8. Do this over and over and over again until it comes true.

Now that you have shifted one thought that's holding you back, you may have several thoughts that also need shifting. Repeat these steps for each critical thought about yourself, dating, men, and/or relationships.

Transforming your thoughts is a discipline you learn by taking the time to practice it. As you are developing different skills to gain aptitude, this practice is a must. It will save you from those pesky, dark thoughts we all have. It could potentially keep you from sabotaging a good relationship. Trust me, the positive thoughts feel better and lighter. During my long-distance relationship with Stefan, the new thoughts I reminded myself of daily—and I mean daily—were: *"We are great together," "My life will be better with him in it," and "He is my playmate and teammate."* It all came true. My new thoughts led to taking new actions that made the difference in this relationship. I recommend developing and flexing this muscle around your thoughts now, so when your fulfilling relationship arrives, your muscle is well trained to keep these positive thoughts alive and strong.

Practice #7

The Busted "Man-Picker"

"Life finds its purpose and fulfillment
in the expansion of happiness."

—Maharishi Mahesh Yogi

When you've been in unhealthy relationships before or chosen people who weren't good for you, it's common to feel like your "picker" may be off. Do you feel like your "man-picker" is busted? This can cause you not to trust your ability to choose a good partner. Of course, you may be hesitating in some way to date or get into another relationship. Dating and realizing you've picked wrong, then taking breaks from dating and wanting to be in a relationship, then dating again and picking wrong again can be a frustrating, vicious cycle. Oh, have I been there! You also may be feeling a bit confused. This practice will help you clarify who you are looking for from a new and different perspective. Practicing it will make your man-picker better and more effective. It's a great tool for weeding out lousy partners. It keeps you from getting stuck in previous patterns so you now select amazing potential partners. Are you ready for some clarity?

As human beings, we each yearn to be in relationship with another person. Yet, based on past decisions, we let doubt set in or believe our skill in choosing someone great has become weak. Consider how many times someone has asked you, "What kind of person are you looking for?" In response, you rattle off a list of qualities you want. When I was single, I got sick of hearing that question from my married friends. I even started avoiding them because I did not want to answer it. It felt as if I were broken. If you are feeling the same way and you still don't have the kind of cherishing and loving relationship you want, then this practice is for you.

This particular activity helps you look from a different and fresh perspective, perhaps a brand new point of view you haven't yet considered. As you think about the type of man you want to spend the rest of your life with, put your attention on you for a minute and ask, "As a woman, what kind of man would make me feel fulfilled for a lifetime?" I'm calling this new perspective your "fulfillment list".

For example, on my fulfillment list was someone who loved to travel. He also had to be a fun and adventurous travel partner. I didn't want someone boring or stressed out when traveling. I wanted someone who liked to travel and could laugh with me if we got lost. Also on my list was someone who enjoyed personal growth and development work. He would be someone who liked to participate in learning as an individual and participating in seminars together. In addition, I knew hands down I needed a partner who was reliable. Flaky and unreliable people make me bonkers. They are a distraction. Finding a man of integrity was big on my list.

I also had to confront and examine some tougher issues, such as children. I realized for myself that I'm not interested in having children. I considered many things like my age, my freedom, and the lifestyle I want now. I have no qualms about it. I love kids and think they are very special, and I know I'd be a great mom. However, over the last several years, I came to a decision not to have children of my own, unless the higher power intervened and I unexpectedly got pregnant. If that happened, I'd embrace the opportunity to raise children and have a family. As I was seeking a great partner, one of the things I included on my fulfillment list was a gentleman who did not have or want children. It's okay to say what you truly desire. There are a lot of women who want children, and they absolutely should have them. There are women who would be happy raising someone else's children and not having some of their own, and they should have that. There are also a lot of women these days choosing not to have children. My point is you deserve to have exactly what you hunger for, so be strong enough to stand your ground for your own fundamental requirements, wishes and preferences.

Yes, there can be some compromises. For example, I craved a partner who had a deep spirituality. Stefan is not religious. However, his way of being, the way he treats others, and our daily practice of gratitude are all very much in line with my spiritual beliefs. Most importantly, we discussed these things early on.

These are a few examples to get you started. The fulfillment list shouldn't be long. Consider the list as characteristics a man should have for *you* to be *fulfilled* and wanting to spend time with him. You would also want to spend your emotional energy on him. My clients have heard me say that I recommend people date for *quality* versus quantity. Your time is precious. Don't waste it dating people who are clearly not for you.

Take a few minutes to write down your fulfillment list. Most of the time, this list should include five to ten items. My clients often ask, "Is this what you are looking for?" or "Did I do this right?" The beautiful thing about your fulfillment list is that it's *yours*. Only you know what will fulfill you. You may need to dig deep, as this isn't a question you hear every day. Being specific about it is the gift you give yourself. No one knows better than you.

Now that you've written your list, glance at it and ask yourself, "*If I met someone with all of these qualities or even 80 to 90% of them, would he be someone I could be in a long-term, healthy relationship with? Is this someone I would want to get to know and give my time and emotional energy to?*" Are you willing to have 100%? If the answer is yes, you have put together a valuable list for yourself. If your answer is no, take a couple minutes to think bigger and revise your list. There are times I stop and think about my current relationship with Stefan and wonder, "*How on earth did I meet someone who is such a great match for me?" I never thought a partnership could be so easy and flow like this. I'm so lucky and grateful to have done the work on myself to have this kind of love and life.*

Your task now is to keep your own personal fulfillment list in a place where you can easily access it. If you start seeing someone and they have 20% or 40% of this list, you may want to ask yourself, "*Is this person someone I really want to spend my precious time with?*" If not, you may want to call him and end it, so someone more suitable can come into your life. I am finding in my work with people that those in good, solid and lasting relationships have about 80% or higher of this list actualized. I often ask my clients who have found potential partners, "Does he meet most of your fulfillment list?"

In my opinion, for relationships these days to have a good shot at lasting, they must be fulfilling in those key areas that are important to you. Some people will have some of the characteristics you are looking for, and they may surprise you with things you didn't know you were looking for. Are you willing to be surprised and have even more? If you look back on some of your ex-boyfriends or ex-husbands, can you see now why it didn't work out? Can you see why you didn't feel completely fulfilled? Our past does give us great insight into who we like to be with and who we don't.

Just don't let it stop you from finding someone who really has you feeling truly fulfilled and delighted.

One of my clients had attributes on her list like unconditional love, kindness, patience, generosity with no strings attached, and listening. The man she is about to marry has all those things.

A new client just made a list: a man who is responsible for himself and his emotions, is a fun travel partner who appreciates the arts, is generous, cleans up after himself in every way, is a reliable partner, and is kind and welcoming to her grown children. Will she find him? We don't know, yet. At least now she has defined for herself the key areas that would have her feel fulfilled as a person and as a woman in a relationship, so she'll know it when she sees it.

Here are the steps to this practice:

1. Consider the characteristics a man would have to have for you to feel fulfilled in your relationship with him. Another way to ask this question is, "What type of man would make me feel fulfilled for a lifetime as a person and a woman?"

2. Write down a list of five to ten key characteristics he should have. This is your fulfillment list.
3. Keep your list where you can check it often.
4. As you meet men and date, refer to your fulfillment list and see if the man you are with has at least 80-90% of those characteristics. Do not waste your time dating men who do not have the possibility of leaving you fulfilled and happy.

He is out there, and now you have done the work to be able to identify him. Congratulations on taking a great step toward having clarity, seeing him when he arrives, and, ultimately, being with him!

Practice

Now, Not Later

"A successful life is one that is lived through understanding and pursuing one's own path, not chasing after the dreams of others."

—Chin-Ning Chu

Have you ever put off doing something because you are waiting for that romantic partner to do it with? Are you currently waiting to do something like eat at a special restaurant, try a new activity, or travel until *he* arrives? I did that, especially in the area of travel; that is, until I attended the launch for Kristen Moeller's book Waiting for Jack. It is about the futility of putting your life on hold. I remember sitting at a table with a good friend and several people I didn't know. We were asked to do a group exercise about what we were waiting for in life. One of the things I shared with the group was that I was waiting to travel until I had a romantic partner to go with me. It's funny what happens when you have to express your thoughts out loud. I realized the absurdity of my statement and said, "I'm not going to wait any longer! This is my life—my one and only precious life."

Shortly after the book launch, I booked a plane ticket for one to Maui for four days. I was a little nervous because I had never traveled by myself. I figured Hawaii would be safe and enjoyable because the weather was always warm and I loved the beauty.

While in Maui, I loved basking in the warm water and the views, as well as the comfort of being on my own schedule. I also appreciated socializing with people at the bar, getting to know new people, and retiring to my quarters whenever I wanted. The freedom to be with myself and on my own was a truly delightful gift. I hadn't read an entire book cover-to-cover in forever, and taking a nap in the afternoon was heavenly.

Before I met Stefan, a lot of men were inspired by me. I had quit putting my life on hold and they saw and loved my passion. I was attractive to them because I was happy and fulfilled. Yet, they themselves were still struggling and not happy or fulfilled. I also realized I had more options in the dating market. I learned to say thanks but no thanks. Would you like to increase your options?

If you are waiting to pursue your goals, waiting to do what fulfills you and makes you happy, waiting to do what you love and are passionate about, go for it now rather than later! If you put your life on hold you might miss an opportunity. Besides, if you meet someone who is having a ball in life and following what he loves right now, wouldn't you find that attractive? You'll be more attractive, too, when you're advancing your passions.

This is an exercise to help you continue to create your happy, fulfilling and healthy life now and *not* later. If you are already forwarding your dreams, let's see how you can boost your life to a higher level.

1. Write a list of all the things you love to do. What are you passionate about?
2. Identify and circle two things you love to do that you are not doing today that you'd like to start doing.

3. Take two actions on those things you'd love to do and be sure to put them into your calendar. They might be:
   - Take a dance class or a cooking class.
   - Plan a vacation and buy an airline ticket.
   - Start a new hobby.
   - Go to the gym.
   - Plant flowers.
   - Go skiing.
   - Go hiking.
   - Learn a new language.
   - Join an online dating service.
   - Go see a movie you like. (Yes, by yourself.)
   - Visit a restaurant you've been dying to try.

It's important to start taking steps and doing the things you love because the truth is that when you are pursuing these things, you feel happier. Isn't that a great time to meet someone unexpectedly? Another reason to actively go for the things you love is that you can meet available men who also go to these places and enjoy similar interests. You never know where you will bump into someone, or how much time you have to do what you love, so you may as well go for it now! When an opportunity presents itself, take a risk and jump in. Being available, ready, and fulfilled in your own life are keys to seeing the right person when he shows up.

After my trip to Maui in May, I booked a trip to Cancun, Mexico, in August that same year. I went with a big group of people from around the world through a transformational leadership organization. It was a seven-day vacation that included a training and development course. I almost didn't know where to start to plan for it or what to do with myself because I couldn't remember the last time I had been on a seven-day vacation.

After arriving in Cancun, I settled into my hotel, and got ready for the first dinner. I was still amazed that I was going to be in such a beautiful place for a week. As my roommate and I had wine and dinner at a poolside table, I casually glanced around the pool area.

"I wonder who else is here this week," she said.

"I have no idea how this week will go, but no matter who we encounter, I'm planning on soaking up every moment," I replied.

"Excuse me," a male voice with a German accent broke into our conversation. "May I take one of these chairs?"

I turned my head and found myself gazing up at

a tall, handsome gentleman with striking hazel eyes. "No, and you should sit here," I answered playfully. There were two open seats at our table, and I wanted him right next to me.

"I'm Stefan," he introduced himself. Little did I know this man would end up being *my* man. I spent the rest of the week surprised and blissful as we began getting to know each other.

One of my clients, Donna, gave up waiting and started doing things she loved, too. She had this to say about her experience:

> *"In 1987, I married the man I thought I'd be with for the rest of my life. In fourteen years of marriage, we had two beautiful girls and life seemed perfect—until my husband announced he wasn't happy and left. I was devastated! This was not what I signed up for. What about 'until death do us part'? What was wrong with me? Once the shock wore off, I started to realize just how numb I'd become. This was not a loving, connected, passionate relationship. We were not going to stay together just for the sake of our kids. The divorce was amicable, he is a loving father to our children, and we remain good friends to this day.*
>
> *"So now what? I'm forty, alone, and basically have no life other than being a mom. Some friends took me out and introduced me to country dancing, and a counselor helped me see there was really nothing 'wrong' with me. Before long I got into a*

relationship that lasted about eight months, then one for three and a half years. Nice guys—just not the one. After that, I dated here and there and went for a stretch of time where I didn't date at all. I told myself I just didn't want to mess with it anymore, but I didn't realize how resigned and cynical I had become about dating and men.

"Then came Suzanne's workshop, and I had the breakthrough I wanted within the first five minutes. The workshop was fun and creative, and it gave me a whole new world to live into! Afterward, I actually looked forward to going on a date. I started going out dancing, I experienced a wonderful freedom around men. Fun and play were present for the first time.

"While dancing with an attractive man one evening, I had no idea that he would turn out to be the man of my dreams. I was just doing what I loved to do. However, something about this guy was magical, and we were married six months later!"

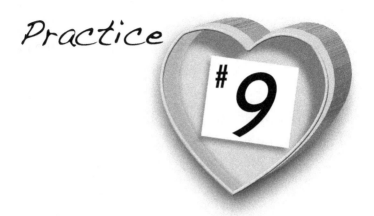

Practice #9

Clutter

"Clean out a corner of your mind and creativity will instantly fill it."

—Dee Hock

While I was searching and yearning for love, a friend gave me a copy of *Feng Shui: How to Look Before You Love* by Nancilee Wydra. At first I was offended and thought my friend wanted to "fix" me. After a few weeks, however, I decided to pick up the book and take it seriously.

Surprisingly, what I found most useful was the concept of cleaning out and organizing my life to make more space for *him* to show up. I understood the concept, but I wasn't a believer yet. Curious to see what might happen, I started throwing things out left and right. I would ask myself, "Do I love this item?" If the answer was anything other than "yes" I gave it to a friend, donated it to a local thrift store, or tossed it in the garbage. All remnants from ex-boyfriends—gone! I was amazed at how much unnecessary stuff I had collected over the years. Was the stuff clogging up my love life? Perhaps.

As I started clearing out, throwing out, organizing and de-cluttering, I was shocked at the benefits I received. My mind became clearer, my heart opened wider, and life seemed simpler, lighter and easier. I even felt more productive and efficient in my life. You may think cleaning out and reorganizing is a big job, and it may be, but I promise, the benefits and rewards are worth it. Let me see if I can help you break it into smaller chunks.

Which room in your house or apartment is the most cluttered? Which closet or cupboard is the biggest mess? Choose one area and take action:

1. Schedule time in your calendar to clean it, even if it's just for a short time, like ten minutes or half an hour.

2. Turn on the radio or grab friends to help. Make it fun.
3. After you've cleaned out a drawer, a closet, or a room, be sure to celebrate your accomplishment.
4. Notice how the energy in the room feels now. How do you feel? Can you sense the change?

At first it may be uncomfortable to give something away that you've had for a long time, but consider that this act is advancing your love life. Once you get started, it may be hard to stop. That is great. It should feel really good as you make progress. You can do it!

Little did I know, two years after clearing my clutter, I'd be moving to Switzerland to live with my boyfriend. My early housecleaning paid off in ways I couldn't even imagine. Packing to move overseas was easier, too! You never know what might happen when you create space in your heart and home. You might not move to Switzerland by doing this practice, but you can be open to other amazing miracles from your efforts.

Practice #10

Learn Your Buns Off

"Tell me and I forget. Teach me and I remember.
Involve me and I learn."

—Benjamin Franklin

School may be over for you, or maybe not, but you can always keep learning. I undertook seriously learning about love and relationships one day when I put a stake in the ground and said, "Enough." I was still on the dating court. Something wasn't working with me, with men, with dating, with love, and with the whole stinkin' process. Enough! It was time to stop the merry-go-round. Why wasn't there a course about this? Oh, wait: there was one—in the school of hard knocks!

Although I wanted to give up on love many times, I knew if I did, I would never accomplish my dream of having a fun and fulfilling partnership in my life. Instead of quitting, I decided to educate myself about men, gender dynamics, dating, healthy relationships, and love. This helped me in taking a much needed look within.

One would think that after seven years of personal development work, I would have had all of this down pat, but no. To tell the truth, I didn't understand men or the male/female dynamic, and I certainly did not understand what a "healthy" relationship was. What is true love anyway? The good news is, with all this training, I became a really great date. However, I was still missing the boat somewhere when it came to going from dating to being in a fulfilling relationship where I allowed the love of a romantic partner in. I wanted a committed relationship more than ever. Even a smart, attractive, and fun woman with common sense would benefit from spending some time learning about men, dating, relationships and love.

I became a closet student, hibernating in my room reading, writing and wondering. I reached for every book I could find. Slowly, some principles sank in, and the light bulb started to shine brighter and brighter! I started doing new things and seeing how men reacted. I felt like a baby putting my big toe in the water for the first time. Instead of viewing men as weak, scary and incapable, I began to see them as amazing human beings. I saw them as these wondrous people who love women, and who love to make us happier. It felt as if I slowly dropped a layer of my independence, and the wall I built up over time had crumbled. Allowing men to actually be of service to me and contribute their love to me was scary. Sometimes it's still a bit scary. The reactions I was receiving from men were different. They seemed to be more interested and attentive, thereby making my life easier and much more fun.

My point is they didn't teach us these things in school, so you may have to do whatever it takes to learn and feel comfortable with these subjects. Here's how:

1. Take a look at this list of areas and see if you can distinguish where you have plenty of confidence and where you feel you don't:
    - Yourself
    - Dating

- Men
- Gender Dynamics
- Healthy Relationships
- Communication
- Playful Flirting
- Love
- Trust

2. Select a handful of topics you want to focus on. Here are a few easy suggestions to help you learn more about the subjects that interest you:
   - Bookmark a good blog or two about the subject
   - Take a class (seminar, teleseminar, retreat, or webinar)
   - Subscribe to a newsletter, or several, on the topic
   - Hire a dating, relationship, and/or love coach
   - Read several books on the subject. Here are some I recommend:
     - *Mastery of Love,* by Don Miguel Ruiz
     - *A Return to Love,* by Marianne Williamson
     - *The Five Love Languages,* by Gary Chapman
     - *Men are from Mars, Women are From Venus,* by John Gray
     - *Calling in "The One": 7 Weeks to Attract the*

Love of Your Life, by Katherine Woodward Thomas

- *Feng Shui & How to Look Before You Love*, by Nancilee Wydra
- *How to Set His Thighs on Fire* by Kate White

3. Create a vision board. A vision board is a fantastic resource because it allows you to do the thinking and create something visual. You can see it every day to remind you of your dreams and the kind of relationship you desire. Here's a link to help you get started: www.makeavisionboard.com/what-is-a-vision-board.html

Seeing how lost I was about men, my former roommate gave me the book *How to Set His Thighs on Fire* by Kate White, the former Editor In Chief of *Cosmopolitan*. I read the book in a couple of days. My jaw dropped time and time again as I discovered what men like and what men need. Bells went off in my head every couple of pages. Not only did I find the book an interesting and fun read, I had no idea I had been saying things to men that turned them off. I would talk about problems I was having at work and areas of my body I didn't like. I would criticize myself in a deprecating way that was beyond laughing at myself.

After much study, dating men became almost effortless and I became more attractive to men. While learning all I could about men, relationships and love, I began to feel loveable; I became irresistible and unforgettable to men, and my confidence around them skyrocketed.

My point is the worst thing you can do is to quit or do nothing. Start to determine where you are uncertain or wobbly. Then learn your buns off. You will be surprised how quickly you can soak up the knowledge and how many resources are available to you. Over time and with practice, your confidence will gain momentum, and you will realize you can have that fulfilling relationship. It'll be worth the investment of your time. If I can do it, you can do it!

Practice #11

Natural Feminine Energy

"Believe in yourself! Have faith in your abilities! Without a humble but reasonable confidence in your own powers you cannot be successful or happy."

—Norman Vincent Peale

Because no one seems to know everything about men and women, one of the best things you can do for yourself is to continue learning. As a student eager to learn, and still a little unsure of myself, I asked men directly what they liked and didn't like in a woman. Inquiring about what kind of women they are attracted to and why allowed me to comprehend what was important to men.

I figured if I wanted to understand a future romantic partner, who better to ask than men? As I interviewed them, I discovered that they wanted me just to be "me," in touch with my own feminine energy. It was simple, but I was not quite comfortable, yet. I noticed that in my *natural* state I already was feminine, fun, happy, loving, nurturing, supportive, and so on. That's what some men are looking for in a woman. On the other hand, some men want a lady who is sweet, knows what she wants, and has a sense of humor. While conducting research for an Ins & Outs of Men teleseminar I was planning for women, I had the opportunity to ask several men in happy, healthy relationships what two qualities they looked for in a partner. Here are their responses:

- Sense of humor and attractiveness: "It is important to have a good time when we are together. I also have to be attracted to her. I have to feel like I could contribute to her and that she would include me in her life."
- Someone who is as invested in the relationship as I am: "Too often I put a lot more time and effort into the relationship than the other person

and that doesn't work. I also want someone who would be able to grow with me and share new things, learn about my favorites, and show me her favorites. Not to say that everything has to line up, but it's good to know what the other person is passionate about, and what they love."

- Someone who likes me and likes men: "I have learned to tune in to my gut and see how I feel around her. Can I be myself with her? Is she present with me? Does she hear what I say? Do I like being with her? Is she fun, interesting and present?"
- Sexy, humorous, smart, and reliable. "I like smart women; they are so sexy to me. It's also important to be able to laugh and have a good time with her, and have a partner who I can work with through the tough times."

What similarities are you seeing throughout? What natural qualities do you have of the ones listed above? Can you see that in your most natural feminine state, you are most or all of these?

The understanding that all men are different and that they are looking for different traits gave me the freedom to be myself and only myself. This new knowledge also provided the opportunity to loosen the load from my shoulders. My job then became to deprogram myself from what I thought men liked and just let myself be my *natural* self. Once I let go of my preconceptions, I could exude my soft but powerful feminine energy. I started exploring life and encountering men who appreciated the characteristics I embodied. As I discovered all of this, things went from difficult to easy to super easy.

I can see now that I had been trying to be someone other than myself so men would like me. I was crossing my fingers that someone would fall in love with me. Gradually, the men I dated would uncover that I wasn't being the real me. I often heard, "Everything about you is great on paper, but something isn't there." The end result was always the same: he would fade away, break up with me, or find someone more compatible. It all makes sense now that I know that when I am being my natural feminine self is when a man can truly love me through-and-through.

Today, my partner loves and adores me for who I am. I don't have to play the "game." I don't have to "get" him to like me. It's such a relief and so much healthier, as well. There is still effort to give to the relationship, but being my best self now makes life a lot more comfortable.

In this next activity, you're going to pinpoint which qualities are naturally you, like happy, friendly, fun, light, sweet, funny, playful, smart, supportive, nurturing, generous, compassionate, silly, adventurous, loving, and so on. In doing so, you'll discover your natural self at a deeper level. Are you ready?

1. First, write down every great characteristic you have. This should be a long list. If you're struggling to recognize your own positive attributes, ask your friends and family to assist you.
2. This handful of qualities is what makes you unique. Once your list is created, star the ones you think best fit you. Look at them again and narrow them down to your top three. Pick the three that you think describe your most natural self. The reality is, there are billions of other women out there (yes, competition), and you must understand what makes you unique. It will also serve as a tool to be sure the man you are with grasps why he is with you and not someone else.
3. Your next challenge is to be those as much as possible. As you meet men, become more comfortable with talking about a couple of the attributes that you have, and let yourself be known for them. Consider it your very own infomercial.

If you say you are fun, and most of the time when you are out with someone you are down and depressed, it's not going to go very well. When you know to your bones what's uniquely wonderful about you, you can be confident in your own skin and understand why he sees you as special. Men don't want to keep looking forever. Actually, a lot of men do want to be in an exclusive relationship with someone who realizes her value and acknowledges her own self-worth. As women, it's up to us to see it first. It makes it even more fun when they acknowledge us for it.

For example, I love being happy, fun and loving, and people know that about me. You may think I'm bragging about being confident in myself, but being bold about what I bring to the table is not bragging. When you clearly understand this, it helps you realize what makes you attractive and special. I love it when my boyfriend says to me, "You are fun to be around." When he tells me this out of the blue, I know I'm being me.

As you are meeting men, dating, and developing that happy and healthy relationship, practice being your natural, divine, feminine self. That's what men are looking for. The sooner you can consistently be comfortable and accustomed to being your beautiful self and loving it, the sooner men will see you as one of those healthy partners they want to snag. Are you open to men flocking to you and your energy?

Words with a BIG Splash

"Being deeply loved by someone gives you strength, while loving someone deeply gives you courage."

—Lao Tzu

When you look at the conversations you have in your daily life, how often do you say the words, "I love you?" Most of us are good at saying, "I love you" to our friends and family, but I'm going to add another way of bringing more love into your life in ways you can't even imagine right now. You'll soon see why this practice works.

People in my life often hear me say things like, "I love your hair; I love that dress; I love the sunshine; I love to travel; I love that restaurant; I love your smile; I love flowers; I love pedicures; I love my awesome boyfriend; I love...." You get the point. I love a variety of things in life, and I express my love about them. If you practice saying "I love..." then saying "I love you" to a partner will become natural when he walks into your life. By saying "I love..." as often as you can, *you* become a love magnet or even a love machine. When men see that you are a loving person, you also become safe to love—you become *loveable.*

The principle behind this practice is that love is a *giving and receiving* phenomenon. The more you give, the more you get. The more you speak love, the more you hear it from others. Those who say "I love..." become more loving and experience being loved. Please don't misunderstand. I don't mean running up to a stranger and professing your love. I'm not suggesting you get ridiculous here. I am recommending that you get in touch with things and people you really appreciate and start expressing love for them.

A great man does listen to what you say and takes notes, especially if he is into you. Trust me on that one. A distracted and unavailable man won't listen, and you'll be able to tell he's not listening. However, most men are listening for what's in your heart and looking for how they might fulfill your heart's desires. If you are not speaking about what you love, they can't pick up the 'signals' and note the things you enjoy in order to give you more.

When you're expressing love in all areas of life, you are exuding loving energy—more than you are aware of. Please note: this practice is not to be used as a strategy to get something. Men can tell when women are being manipulative.

The idea is if you want love to arise, generate love in the air. Even if he isn't the man for you, your time together can still feel good. You don't have to be unkind if the two of you don't "click" with each other. We are all connected in some way. Your paths may cross again sometime, so leaving on good terms is a benefit to your heart and his. If you keep the atmosphere loving and fun, then he will feel much better about being turned down. If you are being your natural and loving self and he isn't interested in going out with you, then you know it's not about you. If it's just not a good fit between you two, it's easier to part ways when you are being loving and kind.

When you are dating and have to break up with someone, it is never easy. I learned to be gentle and kind, yet honest, with men. I've been broken up with many times, and it feels awful. For that reason, when I broke up with someone, I was determined to have him feel honored, respected and appreciated for the good things about him as a man, even though we weren't a good match. Most of the time, he appreciated my sincere honesty, and we both walked away feeling really good about the situation. My heart felt good.

Men love and appreciate the loving, nurturing, supportive, connected, happy, playful energy that women exude. They actually count on it more than we think; they are drawn to it. Women bring a unique dynamic to the mix that men love. When I was conducting my research for my Ins & Outs of Men teleseminar, one man said in his survey, "Women are so different than men. They bring a whole different perspective to things, and they make us feel great when we are with them!"

Remember these words when you are out in life, on a date, in your relationship, or being with a man: "I love…" Fill in the blank—it's a little phrase that can alter everything.

Practice #13

The Love Letter

"Love is composed of a single soul inhabiting two bodies."

—Aristotle

This next practice may seem odd at first, but the impact it will have on your heart is massive. When I was going through my journey to heal my heart after being cheated on, I was down in the dumps. I read Calling in "The One": 7 Weeks to Attract the Love of Your Life by Katherine Woodward

Thomas. She recommended an exercise that m tremendous difference for me. Now, I use it to make that difference for my clients. This practice is writing a love letter to yourself from your future partner. Yes, to *yourself.* Let me explain.

At first I thought this idea was really silly. It felt impossible to even sit down and write such a letter to myself. Consider that this practice is not about you writing a cheesy letter. It's about having to dig deep inside your heart for the words you would like to hear from someone and then writing them into reality. Access to these words comes from a deep place in your soul. When I finally sat down and wrote the love letter to myself from my future partner, I was shocked by the words I typed. They came from a profound part of my heart and made me cry.

Here is my love letter:

Dearest Suzanne,

I'm writing to you because every time I think of you I smile, my heart skips a beat, and if there were butterflies in my stomach they would be fluttering. I still can't believe I met a woman like you; I've looked my whole life and started to think I wouldn't find you. I'm so very grateful that I found you and you found me and we found us. I'm speechless at times when I try to put into words the extraordinary and deep love we have. I never thought it was possible.

I will do everything I can to keep you happy and let you know to your bones that you are loved forever.

I love sleeping next to you every night, hearing you breathe and listening to your heartbeat. I enjoy the intimate life we share. Your body is a masterpiece of beauty. I cherish and adore you. Whether we are talking, playing, walking or connecting in another way, the bond I feel with you is like no other I have ever felt. I want us to spend the rest of our lives together.

I want to be your life partner and share life together forever. I want you to feel safe and protected, and I will do everything in my power to have you feel that way. You have accomplished so much in your life, and I'm so proud of you. I look forward to making a difference, being a demonstration of what's possible, and loving each other, which will in turn provide more love for the world. I want to grow old together, laughing, communicating, and loving each other each and every way we can.

You are amazing and the most beautiful woman I have ever met, inside and out. Thank you for being in my life. I want to continue to connect and grow together. I love you.

—Mr. Wonderful

Here's another example from one of my clients who gave me permission to share her heartfelt love letter.

Lovely Gin!

Be safe, My Dear, in our love. Let your guard down and trust that I am the man who will cherish you forever. We have waited so very long to finally have this joy together. Don't second-guess if or why, just trust what we know to be true.

Feel my heart pound with passion when you are by my side. Just the thought of you makes me smile from the inside out. Each day, I wait to see you, to hear your voice, to think that you might be thinking of me. I can remember the loneliness before we met and how I can now never be without you, ever!

You are me, and I am you. My only sadness comes from regret for not having found each other sooner. How sweet now! Let us not look back, but simply revel today in the pleasure of our future. We are the love that we have only hoped could be ours. I will not question but simply rejoice in you in my life.

I am quiet, complete, and satisfied to live in your love. I can only pray that you are pleased to be with me, as well. What shall we do, my Dear? Will we play in the sea, roam the desert, fly in the sky… and make all your dreams come true? Let's spend life together with no regrets, with nothing unsaid, no hope unfulfilled! Tell me your wishes, they shall be my commands. I have no desire but to serve yours.

You are my treasure! Now that I have found you, I will protect and guard you in honor. No one can violate our sacred bond. Vigilant forever, I shall respect our commitment to hold in trust our love until we are no longer of this world.

This is Mary Ann's love letter:

Dearest Mary Ann,

Words cannot begin to express the profound love I have for you. When I wake up in the morning by your side, I reach over to touch you and kiss you. Then I watch you and wonder what dreams are in your head.

I love the way you wonder at the world—pointing out the beauty. When you are with me, you give me the world.

I delight in you. I want to adore and protect you and be your companion, friend, lover and deepest love. I want to talk with you when the sun goes down and when it comes back up. I love your greatness. I see you and want to hold the all of you in my heart.

My mind is made up. My heart has chosen. I want you. In the end of it all, I want you beside me. I love you for the all of it. I want you with me for my life. You amaze me.

Mr. Yours

Now it's your turn.

Writing your love letter:

1. Position yourself in a quiet area.
2. Open a document on your computer or find a blank sheet of paper.
3. Connect to your heart and ask yourself, "What are the words I'd love to hear from my future partner?"

4. Begin to write…
5. Dear ______,

This practice is your opportunity to believe in the relationship you have only dreamed of. If someone once squashed your dream and you wonder if it's still possible, I'm here to tell you it is! If you can dream it and say it, you can have it! Do not let anyone crush your dreams and your idea of a romantic partnership. A fulfilling relationship can be full of fun, ease, tenderness, safety, and thoughtfulness. It is very available to you. This love letter helps you write it and express it so you can believe it and understand what it will *feel* like. I also highly recommend you store the letter somewhere close to you. I kept mine on my computer desktop and read it every week to remind myself of my aspiration. It also served as a gauge for the men I was dating. It was my way of reminding myself never to settle again.

After you have written your love letter, I'd love to see it if you'd like to share it. Feel free to email it to me at loveable@happylivingforever.com.

Practice #14

Surrender

"If you surrender completely to the moments as they pass, you live more richly those moments."

—Anne Morrow Lindbergh

The word "surrender" can cause many thoughts and feelings to arise. The word used to make my skin crawl. I thought it meant being weak, unsafe, out of control, dominated, and even being taken advantage of in a situation I couldn't escape. It terrified me to no end. Yet, I decided to include it in this book, and I don't mean that old interpretation of surrender at all. You may breathe a sigh of relief. Let me explain.

I was moving out of an apartment one day, and a friend came over to help me pack my belongings. She was in a very successful long-term relationship, and I was dating heavily with little success, so I wanted to pick her brain. As we were sitting there putting my clothes into a suitcase I asked her, "What makes your relationship really great?"

"I just surrender," she replied.

I grappled with that response for a while and couldn't quite get my arms around what she meant. She continued to explain until it soaked in and the light bulb went on over my head. I understood what she meant. Surrendering is to trust myself, my partner, and the process. It means I trust the man has my best interest at heart. I also have faith in myself that if something feels out of place, I will speak up and voice my concerns. I feel assured that everything is happening for a reason, and I keep myself *safe*.

As you are preparing yourself and your heart for love, consider the concept of surrender as a goal. It may not come easily for you at first. If you are independent like me, it can be tough. The most difficult part for me was being able to trust myself to be vulnerable, yet stand my ground when necessary. I used to be very suspicious and trusted no one, sometimes not even myself. I walked around incredibly guarded, protective and alone. Surrender? No way!

In this practice, you'll play with the concept of surrender. For example, try on surrendering to the current reality that you are single. Trust that all is as it's supposed to be no matter what your current relationship status is. The good news is you are not stuck in an unhappy relationship. Instead, you have an opportunity to have the best relationship of your life. Surrender to preparing yourself for dating and love. Trust that you'll meet someone special and that true love will blossom. I found a lot of peace when I surrendered to being a great lady with the skills to have a long-term relationship. I hadn't even met someone great yet! There were also times I surrendered to being sad, frustrated and upset while dating. I even surrendered and allowed myself to trust a higher being that he/she would surprise me and reward me with a luscious and magical relationship. I remember telling my mom once, "Mom, I will have one of those fantasy relationships." Now I do. I surrendered to myself and told myself over and over, "I can do this!" *You* can do this, too.

The feelings you might experience in your body include angst, headache, stress or tension. That's when you can tell that you're resisting something. You know the saying, "What you resist persists." When you have these sensations, remind yourself that you are in the game, on the journey, and forwarding your goals. It's okay to be where you are. Feeling defeated can be part of the process; it's what you do with it that matters. I tell my clients to bring a lot of compassion, generosity and love to themselves during this process. Beating yourself up is normal. However, when you approach *surrender* from allowance, trust and compassion, it opens up a greater sense of ease. It makes dating more fun, and finding a great and compatible mate for you simpler.

As you build trust within, self-doubt is inevitable. When doubt creeps in, ask yourself this powerful question:

> *"If I followed my heart, trusted my instincts, and honored myself, what would I do? What would I say?"*

This question will never lead you astray. I often ask myself that same question, and it opens up everything in my life in a good way. As you ask yourself that question, listen and act on what your heart tells you to do. You'll be glad you did.

Now, being in a healthy relationship that I consider very successful, surrendering for me gets easier daily because of the trust we have established with each other. It took some time. Now we are secure in knowing we truly have each other's best interests at heart. As you are meeting and dating men, surrender to the process. Trust you're on the right path, and you will have more joy, fun and freedom to experience the whole partnership, even the uncomfortable parts.

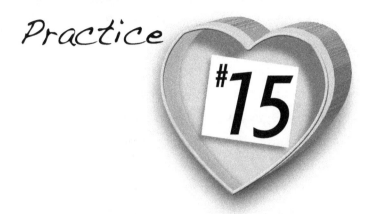

Practice #15

The Art of Playful Flirting

"Success is not final, failure is not fatal:
it is the courage to continue that counts."

—Winston Churchill

Most people are a bit out of practice when it comes to flirting. The word flirting can have some unfavorable connotations, so I'm going to use the words *playful flirting*. Here's why. Playful flirting is a valuable skill when seeking a fulfilling relationship and in keeping the relationship interesting and exciting. It also sounds like a lot more fun, doesn't it? I used to know myself as someone who got bored easily. I liked the beginning stages of dating because I considered it new and exhilarating. Dating new people was exciting and adventurous; then things faded because I relied on the guy I was dating to keep it fun.

Now I know myself as someone who can keep the dating and relationship playful, fun and light. I still think of myself as someone who gets bored easily, which is why I picked an exciting partner. Yes, it is a two-way street, but you can't count on the other person to have the skill, so you must develop it. Again, it increases your *value* to the relationship! Men count on it.

I'm going to give you seven ways to enhance your playful flirting ability. Some of you may be really great at some of these skills, and some of you may want to improve a few of them. I'm talking about flirting now, because these skills are critical in opening the door, finding a wonderful man, and having a lighthearted relationship over time.

If you have been single for a while, many of these playful flirting skills may seem foreign to you. For this reason, I'll go into detail about each. If you are well versed in some of them, practice the ones you would like to take to a whole new level.

#1) Smile: Smiling makes you more approachable. Men will usually approach women who are smiling and having fun. By smiling, you seem safe to men, and they feel comfortable approaching you. No fake smiling, though, because men can sense it. When you are in the relationship, continue smiling. Men love a great smile. Show off those teeth! Smiling is a sign to men that you are friendly, happy and satisfied.

#2) Eye contact: Not just eye contact, but holding the other person's gaze for two to five seconds. Connecting with someone this way often sends a "green light"—the go-ahead to approach you. If you feel awkward holding eye contact, hold it for as long as you are comfortable. Holding eye contact shows your vulnerability and willingness to engage, and it's a great sign to a man that he can come over and speak to you. Don't be afraid to connect with eye contact. Eye contact can create connection and love in an instant. I love looking deeply into Stefan's eyes. I can see and feel his love for me, and it's a beautiful moment. Sometimes words are overrated.

#3) Compliments: Genuine compliments are another great practice. When you sincerely compliment someone, you become someone people like to be around. Who doesn't like a compliment? Do you remember the old saying, "Flattery will get you everywhere"? It's not a strategy, but rather a fantastic art to learn in order to create relatedness with men. The reality is men like someone who makes them feel good about themselves. The idea is to be someone men like to be around and spend time with.

Can't think of anything to say? If they feel natural and sincere, try some of these:

- I like the cologne you are wearing.
- You are a good dancer.
- You have great eyes.
- You have good taste in clothes.
- You are handsome.

Just because you compliment someone does not mean you are going to marry him. It feels good to give compliments, and it feels good to receive them, too. When you are in the relationship, compliments, acknowledgement, appreciation and gratitude will create a warm atmosphere, a safe space and love.

#4) Touch: If you like someone, you have to give him a sign. Men are quite concerned with sexual harassment in this day and age. They can be shy and timid because they do not want to offend you. Consider it their way of respecting and honoring you. If you like a man or want him to know you are interested, gently touch his arm or hand or put your hand on his knee or shoulder. Connectedness is important to a long-term partnership, whether it's holding hands, kissing, rubbing one's back, a hand on the knee, or deeper physical intimacy. Understanding each other's needs in this area will provide joy and comfort.

#5) Ask Questions: Asking men questions about things that interest them is another key to playful flirting. As we have all heard before, men and women are from different planets. Sometimes it's a miracle we even get together at all. Knowing how to grab a man's interest is a key to his heart. Being a woman who asks good questions is sexy. Remember, you are not interviewing him by firing questions at him; rather you're enjoying a nice ebb-and-flow form of asking, listening and savoring good conversation.

Women can fall into a pitfall thinking men are their girlfriends. Men are definitely not your girlfriends. Men don't often want to have the kinds of conversations about shoes, clothes, or dieting that you might enjoy with your girlfriends. Just be aware of how he is responding. You can tell from his facial expressions and how he answers you whether you're on a topic he is really interested in or if you are in the girlfriend territory. That's the part about listening to and trusting your instincts. Kate White's book *How to Set His Thighs on Fire* goes into this in further depth. I highly recommend reading her book for more information about what turns men on and what can turn them off.

Another secret to a man's heart is after asking a question, be interested in his answer. Here are a few suggested questions to ask him:

- What's important to you?
- What do you love to do?
- What makes you happy?

#6) Listen: When you meet someone and you ask him a question, listen keenly. When you listen, trust that you will know the next thing to say. Listening will reduce your nervousness because you are focused on him and not on yourself. Listening is the biggest gift you can give someone. Men look for a partner who will graciously listen to them. Some men believe women talk too much. By limiting your talking and focusing on your listening to him, you can bring a good balance to the conversation. Men will speak when we are quiet, so give them the time and space to speak. Be aware that most men don't speak as much as we do, nor do they like to. On occasion, I'm a big fan of silence. It's actually rather peaceful and nice. I have found I can still be connected to Stefan when we are quiet and enjoying each other in silence. If you find silence uncomfortable, I recommend practicing and learning to savor the quiet with a potential mate. See what happens. It can be a magnetic and beautiful thing.

#7) Laugh: Laughter is a sign you are having fun, which can make you more attractive. If you are out and not having fun, then *be the fun*. It's your assignment then to be someone who knows how to have fun. Men want a woman who can relax, enjoy and laugh. A good sense of humor is appealing. If someone makes you laugh naturally, that's always a very good sign. Wouldn't you like a long-term relationship where laughter is present a lot? I'm a fan of the saying, "How the dating goes is how the relationship will go." If you are laughing and enjoying each other's company from the beginning, the relationship has a great chance of being delightful, entertaining and joyful over the long term.

You can use the playful flirting skills to meet someone great, keep the relationship light and enjoyable, and be a woman who owns who she is. This isn't a one-time skill to land a man; it's an art to practice with your partner, so you can ensure the relationship stays interesting, fulfilling and exciting for the long haul.

Self-Worth

"Only when you are aware of the uniqueness of everyone's individual body will you begin to have a sense of your own self-worth."

—Ma Jian

This subject may be a bit touchy for some; however, it's critical to the process of being loved, loving yourself and being able to completely love a man. In our society, women sometimes suffer from believing they are second to men. Yes, we have made great strides, but this belief is still hanging around. I can hear it when speaking to women. In this practice, let's see how we can conquer this tendency to put men up on a pedestal by further understanding our value.

While dating, I thought the man had all of the control and held all the cards. Over these last several years I've come to realize that *women* have more power than we think. Let me explain.

First, I don't mean women have the power, as in negative force. The days of the bitchy woman are over. I used to think men wanted that type—the bossy woman. I started to believe this because I witnessed couples like that. I pondered, "*Why would he want her?*" It was frustrating to watch couples who were together and the man was at her command. I would watch that dynamic and think, "*All the mean women get the men.*" I tried it, and I failed. I crashed and burned because I'm just not that kind of woman. Let's quash the myth. It's not true that men want to be with a person who habitually criticizes him or tries to change him. However, there is something to be said for a woman who is forthright in her delivery and asks for what she needs and wants.

In my relationship, I now realize my self-worth. I understand what I bring to the table, including fun, love, happiness, playfulness and an equal voice. My past relationships did not go well when I did not speak up or when I would stop saying what I really thought. When I stopped communicating my views, ideas and opinions, I would become meek, distant and small. I realized that what I feel and think matters. Expressing myself is all part of an equal partnership. My current relationship is now full of balance and love because we both recognize that what I bring *as a woman* is very important to the health of the relationship. When I understood this down to my bones, I stopped being afraid to be my powerful self. It changed who I was for myself and for men. Before this, I was just a woman looking for a man and hoping to be loveable.

Back in my dating days, I dated men who weren't a fit for me because I thought they were all I deserved. Yes, they were all good men, but not the right men for me. Over time, I saw that the people I chose to date were linked to my sense of self-worth, and I had been dating down.

Your self-worth is directly correlated to who you think you are and who you think your partner can be. It's also tied to what you believe you deserve, how pampered you can allow yourself to be, and how you speak up. Your low self-worth can stop you *dead in your tracks* and prevent you from dating altogether. Let me show you how.

I was working with a client a few months ago. She had absolutely no idea what she brought to a relationship as a woman, a partner and a person. Her whole dating life was on hold. Understandably, she wasn't even trying to meet anyone. If she attempted to date while having thoughts of "*I'm hopeless*" and "*Men are up on a pedestal*" swirling around in her head, any man would have been able to sense her low self-esteem. Most likely, they would never call her for a second date. A man might say he'd call and then he wouldn't. Sound familiar? While it's not the truth in all cases, it is something to consider. Once she identified what she brought to the table as a partner and shifted her thoughts to "I am his equal and a partner," she saw some new actions to take. She rewrote her online dating profile and posted it. She was actually excited to date.

Men generally want a woman who recognizes her worth and value. In this exercise, you will take your self-worth inventory. Please take out something to write on.

1. Answer the following questions about yourself:
    - What have you accomplished in your life?

- What is your favorite part of your body?
- What makes you a great partner?
- What's your biggest or most recent success?

2. After you've written your answers out, read them over again. What do you notice about your answers? Can you see your value as a woman?
3. This is also a good time to reflect on the top three unique qualities that you wrote down in the natural feminine energy section.

Remember, you are an *amazing woman* with or without a man. As you are dating, keep a cheat sheet with you about *why* you are a great partner, what your value is, and what you can bring to a relationship and a man's life. You may not believe it all right now, and that's perfectly okay. Keep in mind as you are dating and meeting men that a man is someone who can add value to your life and make you happier. Your job is to recognize your highest value as a woman. Well done!

Practice #17

Communication Must-Haves with Men

"My belief is that communication is the best way to create strong relationships."

—Jada Pinkett Smith

Over the years, I've studied communication. I've failed at communication. I've observed communication. I've succeeded at communication. I noticed in my studying and learning that there are several main forms of communication that work while dating and being in a fulfilling relationship. I personally consider communication to be *the key* skill to making or breaking everything. While all of the practices in this book are essential, this particular skill is imperative to your ongoing success.

I often hear women proclaim, "Well, I just want to be me. If he can't handle all of me or me being myself, then maybe I should just be single." I used to say that, too, until I realized I did want a partner. I had to learn how to speak differently to men. Was I changing myself? I don't think so. However, I was shifting, tweaking and altering my language in order to be loveable. It turned out to be fun and thrilling.

You will find these next communication skills valuable in having a relationship that lasts over time. If you are not dating right now, the key is to start practicing with the people around you.

These are the three important types of communication to forward your relationships with men: Forwarding Communication, Straightforward Communication, and Listening to Learn.

1. Forwarding Communication. What's the difference between "Communication" and "Forwarding Communication"? It's easy to criticize. It's easy to judge. It's easy to be grumpy and take your bad mood out on someone.

Whether you realize it or not, when you are down and negative a lot, you drag the energy around you down and men are turned off. These tactics are likely just to get you stuck. What's more, these tactics do not move the conversation with your man forward.

The muscle to build is how to communicate so the conversation is forwarded. As negative and critical thoughts come up, and they will, you must develop the ability to articulate your thoughts productively, to be understood, and to make your dating or relationship situation *better*. Learning to bite your tongue and formulate a thought to constructively express yourself to your man will help you have a fulfilling relationship. Stefan often says to me, "You are very good at presenting something in a positive way through your communication, and that forwards our relationship. I really appreciate that." That's what I'm talkin' about!

How many times have you seen someone say something and bring the whole room down in a moment? Although this person may have meant well, it didn't go as planned. Do you want to do that kind of thing? I doubt it. Words can be very hurtful and can destroy everything you have built in a second. A client shared with me recently, after meeting a new man, "I told him that I didn't want to meet his daughter because this relationship most likely won't work out anyway." As she predicted, they broke up. No surprise. She learned her lesson.

Some questions to ask yourself in the area of communication are:

- *Am I someone who is a safe communicator?*
- *Can someone communicate anything to me?*
- *Do I make the other person feel safe such that they can communicate with me?*

If the answer to any of these is no, you may want to take on being someone who is safe for others to communicate with in your daily life. This is a great practice for anyone. You may be surprised at how much it opens up communication with other people in your life.

Taking an extra minute to consider what and how you are going to say something can save you a lot of time, grief and heartache. Harsh words can lead to discussions that spin the issue into an unpleasant and unnecessary argument.

Here are a few examples:

If you don't like the shirt he is wearing for dinner:

Don't Say: "Are you going to wear that to the party?" (It's undermining and manipulative, not to mention emasculating.)

Do Say: "I love when you wear the yellow shirt. I think you look really fantastic in it."

If you don't like the restaurant he took you to:

Don't Say: "I didn't like the food at that restaurant." (Being critical is inefficient.)

Do Say: "Thank you so much for taking me to that restaurant. The company was the best. I thought the main course was okay and I'm glad we tried it."

Men need positive strokes, and they want to hear compliments just as much as you do—even more, actually. Remember, men do have big egos. If you want a fulfilling relationship, it's critical to express your opinions in a well-intentioned way. He is doing his best to please you and make you happier, so be sure to recognize his effort. While preparing for the *Ins & Outs of Men* teleseminar, one of my male friends who is in a very healthy relationship said, "We are sex-driven, pride-filled, egomaniacs. Work with that fact, don't try to change it!"

Women have learned to be strong, independent, successful, powerful and more. While that's fantastic, men also want to be with a woman who is sweet, happy, supportive, loving in her feminine energy, and a lady. In my coaching and research, this seems to be where women are struggling. The question is, how can you be *both* to get what you want and still have the relationship that you want? Trust me. Using language that's soft but strong can bring harmony, peace and love to the moment instantly.

A few suggestions:

- Think before you speak: How can you communicate your thoughts and *forward* the situation?
- Care about what you say and consider his feelings.
- Consider how you will say it, and then be sweet and loving when you express it.
- Timing is everything, and *when* is a biggie for a man. How and when you bring up a subject with a man can make all the difference.

Considering these four small but important suggestions in your communication will prevent disagreements, hurt feelings and unnecessary arguments. They also keep the dating and relationship situation light, fun and humming along.

We all fail at this from time to time. Remember, apologies go a long way to bring forgiveness to yourself and your partner.

2. Straightforward Communication. Men love and appreciate us women who are straightforward in our speaking because they don't have to guess at what we are trying to say. Men also appreciate it when they don't have to try to read our minds. Once and for all, men are not mind readers, and we cannot expect them to be! Having to try to figure out what we're thinking exhausts them. Again, as I was surveying men for the Ins & Outs of Men teleseminar for women, one man said, "We may be clumsy at times, may not think about others at times, but overall, we simply may need a gentle reminder to get back on the 'couple track'—and it's not personal!"

A woman who can express her needs and wants clearly and unemotionally can make a man very happy because he doesn't have to try to figure out what she is saying. You also must add another ingredient: *sweetness.* What do I mean by this? Men love it when you ask for what you want; however, *how* you say something or ask for something comes into play here and makes all the difference in the world. An example would be: "Make me a cappuccino," or "I need a cappuccino." He will not take that very well. Instead, try saying: "When you have a minute, would you mind making me a cappuccino?" and he will react well to that. A good rule of thumb here is *never ask for something when you are upset and annoyed.* Take time to calm down, and then ask, or preface your request with something like, "I am upset right now, and this may not come out well."

It took me a long time to get the hang of this practice, but now I'm confident in how to speak to my boyfriend. Having built this muscle makes my life such a breeze. Men want to serve you, protect you, and make you happier, much more so than you realize. You have to speak to them from a place of love, sweetness and respect. When you do, watch how they respond. Another man I surveyed said, "Men do want to please women, a lot. Men are so happy to be able to please." I read that a big reason a man will leave a woman is that he can't please her, so he looks for a woman he can please. For example, if he brings you that glass of water, the words *thank you* better be at the tip of your tongue. It seems weird to have to say this, but you would be surprised how many women aren't appreciative. This makes men feel as if they are taken for granted, and they lose heart.

Keep being candid and straightforward in expressing your needs and wants, but don't forget to add that little extra—that sprinkle of sweetness that comes from a loving place. A man loves pleasing his woman. Remember to be the kind of woman he wants to continue to make happier. You may not get everything you want, but what if you received some or most of it? Are you willing to try to add the secret ingredient: sweetness? As a male friend so eloquently put it, "When your spouse respects you, you will die for her." Can you be that kind of woman?

He loves giving to you. Be sure to give him what he needs in the way of appreciation, respect and gratitude, *especially* if his love language is words of praise. Yes, physical attraction is important; however, being loved, loving and loveable also begin with your words. Communication truly is the key to his heart.

3. Listen to Learn. I love the world of listening. It's a fascinating subject. Being a smart listener is another necessary part of success. I've mentioned it before, but in this next practice, I'm going to address listening from a different perspective. Has someone ever communicated something to you that was a bit alarming, so you disregarded it instead of addressing it? Perhaps you just let it slide to be "nice" and it came back to bite you in the butt later. I've done this, and it has caused me discomfort and regret.

Let me distinguish the practice of *listening to learn*. I don't mean listening to catch people to prove them wrong or listening from suspicion. I don't mean listening just to be nice and polite, either. Hardly! I believe everything you need to know about someone will be expressed by them. The question is, are you in the moment and listening enough to be able to hear it? That's the key!

Let me expand. While dating, and even when you're in a great relationship, you are always learning about the person. You are listening to their stories, their past, what they like, what they don't like, and their complaints, among other things. It's crucial to keep your ears wide open. You are looking for a life partner, and everything that comes out of his mouth is relevant.

When I was with the man who cheated on me, there were subtle hints. I just didn't want to hear them because I was in love with him, so I turned a deaf ear. My intuition tugged at me, but I brushed it off, over and over again. In the end, when it came out that he was also in serious relationships with many other women, the person I was most upset with was me. I knew something was odd, but I didn't want to acknowledge it. I ended up wasting a lot of time staying with him, besides making myself nuts with frustration.

Here is another example. I met a tall, hunky, and really fun man on an online dating site. We had a lot in common, and the kissing was like fireworks. We laughed until our stomachs hurt. Our dates were an absolute blast. We had a very easy flow when we were together. On our second date, at a baseball game, we were kidding around about meeting online. He turned to me and said, "If you ever meet my family, you can't tell them we met on an online dating site."

I didn't think anything of it at the time. I may have made a face because I didn't want to rock the boat. I discounted the comment because he was cute and fun, and it was the best time I'd had on consecutive dates in a very long time. However, I should have addressed it then and there because it was a forewarning.

First, I am a dating coach, and I support online dating as a way to meet someone. Second, he was already asking me to lie because he didn't have the nerve to share the truth with his family. Not good. What kind of a relationship does he have with his family? Also, I could tell he was embarrassed about meeting online, which could have been a concern that his confidence was lower than I thought. Maybe he was teased by his big family and wanted to avoid further humiliation at their hands. I will never know because I didn't ask him—shame on me. Shortly after our fifth blissful date that week, the text messages stopped. Something was off. He called a few days later to break up with me because he said the hour-and-a-half drive was too much for him. I was shocked, and yet I was grateful he had the courage to pick up the phone to call and tell me rather than leave me hanging. Did his desire not to let anyone know we met online have anything to do with him breaking things off? I don't know, and it doesn't matter now. I learned to clarify things in the moment—quickly, gently and simply.

This is a small example, but my point is *listen to learn*. A man will tell you everything you need to know about him if you just listen. It's also a good time to point out that he is learning about you as well. Don't be sloppy with your words. He is always interpreting what you say, too. Listen to learn and address things as soon as possible. You do not want to be caught off-guard later because you didn't listen. Discuss issues as you go, early and often. Remember, tone of voice is crucial when communicating with a man. Listening is a huge part of communication. By shifting your current communication style slightly and taking on some new communication techniques, you can have everything you need as a woman, and leave your man wanting more.

Practice #18

Happy & Healthy Couples

"Love is knowing you are the bud
from which his happiness blossoms."

—Source Unknown

When I was single, I was always talking about my dates, good and bad, with my single friends. It was a common conversation, yet it didn't seem to help me be successful. Why did talking to my single friends never result in finding a fantastic relationship? Because the language we spoke back and forth was only in the realm of "single speak." Unfortunately, it kept me on the merry-go-round of being single—the constant circling and being unable to move from the dating scene into a phenomenal relationship.

If this is where you are in your journey, you may feel stuck in a swirl and frustrated like you can't get out. It could almost feel like you are drowning. I have been there. Here is another way I made the jump from dating to an unbelievable relationship.

A very wise course leader once told me, "Suzanne, if you want a healthy and happy relationship, stop talking with single people about your dating and man issues. Speak to people who are in the kind of relationship you want." The bell went off—*ding*! I quickly realized I love my single friends dearly. However, our conversations were not constructively forwarding my goal to be in a healthy and happy relationship. I stopped having "single speak" conversations with them. I spoke to my single friends about many other topics, but the conversations about men and dating just weren't working. When they asked me how my dating life was going, I said, "Good," and changed the subject to something else.

On my drive into work back in my corporate days, I would ring up one friend who had the kind of relationship I desired. I loved listening to her talk about her relationship with her boyfriend. Often, I drooled over her success, and over time I started soaking in the language she so beautifully articulated. I then started mimicking her. Maybe I was a copycat, but slowly I shifted my ways of behaving and being around men. I modified how I acted around them. I altered what I said to them. I even shifted who I was for myself. This transformation can be rapid or it can take time, so be generous and compassionate with yourself. You most likely will fail at first, as I did. That's perfectly natural. The practice is what makes you proficient.

I also recommend not hanging out with couples who have unhealthy relationships. It can serve as a deterrent to your goals. If you do, at least recognize those couples do not have the kind of relationship you have your eye on. I figured if a happy and healthy relationship is what I hungered for, then I should mirror people who already had it. It worked very well.

Here is an exercise to learn more about healthy relationships from the people who are in them.

1. Observe healthy couples. Try to see if you can take on their mannerisms.
2. Interview couples who are in the kind of relationships you want. Take mental notes.

3. Shadow someone who is in a relationship that you admire. What does the person do and say? How does this person act and behave with her partner? Watch how he responds to her.
4. Build relationships with people in great relationships. Be a student and learn, learn, learn.

As you connect with happy couples that you admire and respect, consider doing this exercise from the perspective of a student. You are learning from people who have what you want; shadow them. Don't worry; it won't take long before you get the hang of it. Consider it your very own master's course on dating, men, relationships and love. Soon you'll be someone who others enjoy mirroring because you are in a great relationship that's playful and tender.

Practice

Spoiled and Pampered

"Where your pleasure is, there is your treasure:
where your treasure, there your heart;
where your heart, there your happiness."

—Saint Augustine

Do you love to be spoiled? Do you love to be pampered? Do you love to receive? We women do. However, we can be a bit rusty at letting men treat us to these pleasurable things. In reality, we have been trained to give, give, and give some more. Yes, being nurturing is part of our DNA, but there is a shift happening in today's day and age. It's about being treated like a princess and thoroughly enjoying it! Men do love to do these things for us. Are you willing to be cherished, adored and treated like a princess? If not, let's look at what may be stopping you.

Have you ever been trained to let a man take you shopping and cater to you? Have you been prepared to sit and just enjoy a man cooking for you? Have you learned to receive an hour-long body massage or neck massage without feeling guilty? My guess is no, or not really. You probably have not been trained to receive anything that feels indulgent. Welcome to the club. I had to learn it, too. Now I know that it's a fantastic way to live. I had no idea what I was missing! Of course, there is a give and take that's needed. But my point is, can you really receive? Receiving is a form of accepting love.

Whatever the reason you struggle with being comfortable receiving from a man, this next section will help you practice accepting pampering and being spoiled, not as an expectation but as a possibility.

I'm not just speaking about men treating us to these nice things; I'm also talking about treating ourselves to them. Accepting this kind of treatment is a gift and an act of love. Treating yourself to a day of reading, relaxation, and the spa is a gift you give yourself. When is the last time you managed to delight in an amazing day of shopping, a pedicure, and a massage to thank your body for all it does for you?

As an independent woman, I often thought in terms of "I can do it myself" and "I don't need you." I had no problem making really good money and paying my own bills. In fact, for just over forty years, it's all I ever knew. Although I was successful, I was still lonely and unfulfilled. I thought I had to keep it all together. One day I realized, if I wanted to be a partner who could accept contribution from a male partner, I might need to give up some of that independence and allow a man to be generous to me. The thought almost made me sick, but I knew something drastic needed to change. The process took rearranging every molecule I had in my body to be able to receive a man's love in different ways, including financially, emotionally, and physically. I thought I would lose who I was. Instead, I felt his love from a different perspective. In being able to receive, I felt more self-love and fulfillment in new ways.

Here are a few suggestions:

1. When a man offers to do something nice for you, say, "Yes," and then say, "Thank you."
2. Don't think you have to give back or keep score if a man gives to you. I call this the "Reciprocate

Equally Syndrome." It will start to feel terrible if you sense he is giving you something to get something, or even if you feel like you always have to answer every contribution from him with something equal. If this starts to occur, have a conversation with him about each of you only giving to one another from the heart. It's okay not to give if that giving is not truly from the heart.

3. Appreciate his ways of contributing to you. It may not look the way you think it should look. Be grateful for his effort.
4. Give up the idea that you don't deserve to be pampered. That's a self-defeating context.

One of my coaching clients, Jill, had this experience dating a man when she allowed herself to receive pampering and spoiling.

> *"Kevin took me to a five-star steakhouse for our first date and invited me to his wine locker to choose our dinner pairing. He treated me like a princess the entire night and told me during dinner that I was the first woman he ever reached out to online. He said he knew a good thing when he saw it, so he wanted to see where this would go. As I'm writing this, I look down to my buzzing phone. It's Kevin planning our second date. 'Jill, how does this sound? I will pick you up tomorrow at 2 for a ride through the mountains in my convertible. Then we can stop by your house so*

you can change clothes and freshen up before dinner. I'm thinking lobster, steak and a great red wine. Is that good for you?' Is Kevin the one? I don't know yet, but what I do know is this. I shifted my thoughts, I elevated my feminine side, and I'm being my genuine self every moment, and the result is that I'm attracting a different type of man. I'm attracting men who are kind, thoughtful, emotionally mature, successful and in service of me."

Nurturing yourself and treating yourself to a good spoiling and pampering is another way to be able to accept a man's love and contribution. It takes practice. If you can't grant yourself love, how can you expect it from a man? Be good to yourself, and a great man will enjoy showering you with love and thoughtfulness. When you can enjoy his acts of kindness and ways of expressing his love, adoration and amazement of you, you'll delight in the art of being spoiled and pampered.

Practice #20

Expectations

"Happiness cannot be traveled to, owned, earned, worn or consumed. Happiness is the spiritual experience of living every minute with love, grace, and gratitude."

—Denis Waitley

One of the hardest lessons I learned from my past was to give up my expectations. It seemed as though every time I held an expectation of men, it never went the way I thought it should. I would quickly fall into being disappointed, annoyed and let down. I knew these beliefs were not serving any purpose in the situation, but I couldn't seem to shake them. I was stuck—attached to things going a certain way—and easily frustrated. Whoever I was dating at the time would realize my expectations were so high, they were almost impossible, Men were doomed from the get-go, so they fled.

After numerous men made a mad dash out my door, hoping to find a woman they could please, I initiated the *zero* expectations philosophy. It worked like a charm. Let me explain.

First of all, I don't mean you should have low expectations. Having any expectations at all is like putting a box around the situation, the experience, the outcome, and the man. If your expectations are already small or average, or coming from the past, and not what is truly possible, you're limiting your own experience. That's not what I'm talking about. I'm saying relinquish *all* of your expectations.

One evening when I was in my early forties, I was preparing for a date. I had met a gentleman online and we were to meet at a nice restaurant in downtown Denver. Being five feet, eleven inches myself, I was very excited to meet this tall, handsome man. Yet, as I was curling my hair, I thought to myself, "*Another first date. Ugh, I'm getting tired of first dates.*" I could almost predict how a first date was going to play out. In the next moment, however, I asked myself, "Suzanne, what if you had no idea how a date should look? What if you had no idea how a first date would go?" I gave up my predictions about it. Sure enough, we had a fantastic time together, laughing and strolling along the streets of downtown Denver. After a spontaneous kiss goodnight, which was a really nice treat, I drove myself home in bliss, glowing from being pleasantly surprised by all the things I didn't expect. It was one of the best first dates of my life. Well, it was one of the best until I met Stefan and we swam with the dolphins.

When I relinquish any and all expectations, I'm usually baffled at how my life turns around beautifully. Things happen far better than I could have ever imagined or thought. It's like taking the box off altogether or busting down the walls of the box completely. Life becomes about being in the surprise of the moment. Life becomes about being in *awe*.

When I started to live in the amazement of the moment, more happiness arose as well. Slowly, I was able to rearrange my thoughts and live in the pure joy and happiness brought about by a man's efforts. Men are fantastic human beings when you allow them to be.

The power of having zero expectations is allowing for the unexpected. What if things could actually be *better* than you anticipated? What if you let a man be his greatest self and surprise you in ways you couldn't imagine? What if you learned to silence your mind and just enjoy the moment, no matter how it presents itself? This is when all the *magic* happens.

Ways to Quiet Your Mind:

1. If you have to-do items for the next day that make your mind wander, schedule them in your calendar or write them down and put them aside. They will always be there tomorrow.
2. Focus on listening to the other person. Be curious about what matters to him.
3. Take a few deep breaths before going out. Calming the body will calm the mind.
4. Bask in the awe of the human being sitting in front of you. This can remove some of the nervousness and "what ifs".
5. Dismiss any thoughts of the past and rein your mind in from imagining the future. Be in the now! If memories of an ex are coming up, take a few minutes and revisit the Lighten the Load exercise in Practice 2.

This isn't an easy skill to develop. However, by using these simple suggestions, over time you can quiet your mind and enjoy the moment. What if the unknown is really exciting? What if being in the moment provides more than you could ever imagine? All of these practices can also increase your level of trust in yourself and in men. Are you willing to date in the experience of awe, magic and excitement? Take on zero expectations and watch your life become more fulfilling as a result.

Practice #21

Thank You

"Gratitude unlocks the fullness of life. It turns what we have into enough, and more. It turns denial into acceptance, chaos to order, and confusion to clarity. It can turn a meal into a feast, a house into a home, a stranger into a friend."

—Melody Beattie

I saved "Thank You" as the final practice on purpose because it's one of the most powerful and effective practices in the bunch. Consider it as saving the best for last. Most people think you should be thankful when there is something to be thankful for. That's backwards. Gratitude is your ticket to a juicy partnership and the best life ever. As a society, we can be stingy. It actually takes a powerful and confident person to be the one who generates gratitude first, even when you don't know if you will receive it in return.

First let's define what gratitude isn't. It's not a strategy to receive something. It's not a sign of weakness. It's not a way to get something in return. It is not hard.

When Stefan makes me a cappuccino in the afternoon, I always thank him for his generosity, although it's almost a daily thing. I never take it for granted. He doesn't have to make me a cappuccino every day. He does it to show his love for me and he also knows it makes me happy. I am always aware of my words of gratefulness, and I try to give them as often as I can. Of course, I would love to have more cappuccinos in my future, and I don't take it lightly that he whips them up almost every day. I want him to know how I appreciate them and him.

Gratitude is strictly a way of keeping the wonderful things in your life flowing. It also feels good. When you are grateful for something, you can receive more in your life. Besides, men crave appreciation. They need to know they are respected and admired.

I dated a gentleman for a short time a while back who told me something that has stuck with me over the years. He said, "Sometimes, Suzanne, you have to give to get." He didn't mean to "give" as a strategy. He meant that I was being guarded with my words, holding back, and expecting something. He was telling me to stop waiting for someone to give it to me before I gave it. At first, receiving that feedback stung a bit. I was ashamed of being so stingy. After a moment, though, his message landed powerfully in my heart.

By shifting my behavior, giving compliments freely, and appreciating the small things, my life swung dramatically the other way. I exchanged being critical for being grateful and finding the good in men. After my gratitude muscle became stronger, men loved being around me. They loved my energy, they loved how I made them feel, and they loved my attitude. Today, my boyfriend often tells me, "Suzanne, you are so much fun to have around." Those words make my heart sing because I know I'm being my true and best self, and he notices.

How can you open the floodgates of generosity? Would turning up the gratitude knob benefit you in your life? Generosity in this sense has nothing to do with paying for things and giving monetarily. Words are free and priceless, and they make a big difference. Yes, surprising someone by treating is nice at times, as well.

Here are a few key phrases to start your gratitude fountain flowing with ease and grace.

- I appreciate when you…
- I appreciate X about you…
- It makes me happy when you…
- I'm grateful for…
- Thank you for…
- I love when you…
- I love X about you…

Try these simple statements and see how this practice changes your dating life, love life, and overall experience of life itself!

Conclusion

"A loving heart is the beginning of all knowledge."

—Thomas Carlyle

Now that you have completed the practices in this book, you may be considering jumping back into the dating world because you have new ideas, tools and clarity around what you really want. You may have started dating someone new who fits most of your fulfillment list, and maybe even more. You might be in a fantastic, exciting relationship that's just getting off the ground. Wherever you are, I hope you found some new ways to think and developed some skills to take with you. I hope you've developed a muscle that expands your current ability to be Loveable—loved by a man, and able to completely love a man while loving and honoring yourself. These three things should make your dating and relationship experience, and even life, more fun and fulfilling. They, along with the practices in this book, are the real keys to the kingdom!

Do you remember the starting point survey in the very beginning? Before we conclude, let's revisit the survey and check your progress:

1) How much do you trust men?
2) How comfortable are you in the dating process?
3) How beautiful do you think you are?
4) What is your ability to have a healthy relationship that could last a lifetime?
5) How confident are you that you can have a man who adores, cherishes, loves and even worships you in a healthy way?
6) How much do you love and honor yourself?
7) Where would you rate your ability to accept and receive love from a man expressed in emotional, physical and financial ways?
8) How much do you trust yourself?
9) How would you rate your communication skills for maintaining and sustaining a healthy relationship?
10) How would you rate yourself as a great date?
11) What is your ability to make men feel great about themselves?
12) In life right now in general, what is your level of happiness and fulfillment as a person?

How were your results? Higher than before? Lower than before? You should see quite a bit of progress if you have completed each exercise over time and practiced them in your life. If you haven't, it may mean you are in a "next" phase. For example, you weren't dating at all, and now you're dating; or you were dating, and now you're in a healthy relationship. These "next" phases can cause the survey to dip again. Please take the survey as many times as you'd like. The goal is to be in the eights, nines and tens across the board so you are confident that your skills in these areas are solid and strong.

Congratulations on your progress, your success, your new steps, your miracles, and the new skills that you've taken on. Mostly, congratulations on being committed to having the relationship you desire and to being happy. You should be very proud of yourself that you loved and honored yourself enough to try something new. You followed your heart to this book.

Thank you for being on the journey of dating and meeting quality people, working toward happiness, fulfillment, healthy relationships and love. It takes courage and tenacity to sit down, do these exercises, and practice them. They aren't for the faint of heart; they are for someone who truly is committed to having the most fulfilling relationship of their life and have it last—You.

This book is written for women, but don't worry! My next book will be geared for men. When I explain this book to people in a group, the men often pipe in and say, "I want that book." Trust me, they understand that their skills could be refined and upgraded as well. They do want to please us and often don't know how, so please be a loving woman who can point them in a good direction with your natural feminine energy. If he isn't the right fit for you, gently put him back into the dating pool and wish him well. We all want to find that beautiful connection with someone. You can leave someone better off for having known you.

You may be experiencing a lot of success, seeing small accomplishments, or not feeling successful yet. Just know the practices leading to a great relationship are here; keep learning your buns off through the other great resources available. The beautiful thing about this book is that you can redo the exercises at any time to take your skills to a whole new level. You may have just scratched the surface, or you may have opened a whole new destiny that you are excited about and fulfilling on. You will be surprised to see what happens when you revisit the exercises and think a little bigger. Remember, I had to do the new destiny exercise three times before I met Stefan.

If you hit a bump in the road, recognize it as part of the process. If you have a dream, wish and desire to be in the best relationship of your life, you can get there using these practices and exercises. They are meant to steer you toward your goals and have you be happy, healthy and fulfilled. I hope by now you are waking up every day, pinching yourself and saying, "This relationship is unbelievable. It feels too good to be true." It *is* true. What if it keeps getting better every day because you have those zero expectations, and you are staying in the moment? If you haven't met your partner quite yet, know that you will!

Many women I speak to want to be married. Some just want to be in a healthy long-term relationship. Whatever your dream, it can happen. Keep those thoughts aligned and positive, and yourself empowered. You are a fantastic woman; be confident about what you bring to the table as a great partner. Never lose sight of the main qualities you possess that make you unique and wonderful.

I'm so grateful you chose this book and did the work. You are a loveable and amazing woman! Be with a man who allows you to honor yourself, makes you happier and values the gem that you are. You are your best self in your natural feminine energy, so don't be afraid to let it shine!

I would love to hear your comments about the book. What was your favorite practice? Let me know what has shifted for you as a result of practicing these new skills—no matter how big or small. What else would you like to learn about? You can contact me at loveable@happylivingforever.com

If you think you could benefit from some additional personal coaching, please contact me at:

loveable@happylivingforever.com
or
www.happylivingforever.com

Thank you for being Loveable!

Afterword

By now, you may be in a fulfilling relationship. If so, YAY!! You may be dating or just now getting your feet wet. Either way is great. Congratulations for taking steps towards your deepest desires and goals. Now that you have prepared yourself and your heart for the sometimes turbulent dating world, you can feel proud that you are ready! I commend you for doing the work for yourself and being a healthy partner for someone, and opening up the possibility of attracting a loving partner to you. It may take a few dates, lots of dates, or he may walk right up to your dinner table and say, "Hello." Your heart is available, and bigger and wider than ever. You are more loveable—able to love another, able to be fully loved and able to honor and love yourself.

Hopefully, by reading this book you have uncovered more love within yourself and increased your skills to have the most fulfilling relationship of your life. You have also developed the muscle to follow your own heart, trust your instincts and honor yourself. I'm proud of you for gaining the capacity to be clear about who would fulfill you and for being able to shift your thoughts in a moment if they go south. I applaud you for developing the skills to be successful and, most importantly, being able to embrace the kind of relationship that's worthy of your time, money, heart and emotional energy.

Remember Brenda, who has been single for a long time: "Now that I know what I am searching for, the dating process is a matter of the quality of connections I can make rather than the quantity of attention or acceptance I receive, so my fears of rejection have lessened hugely. I am now looking for someone I can be happy with instead of hoping that all the men I meet will like me. By going through the exercises and doing the homework, I have let go the regrets and self-criticism I had built up over the years. My self-confidence has improved immeasurably. I am really looking forward to meeting my future partner. In the meantime I am having fun talking to strangers and being the real me in all company."

Remember Shannon, the single mom: "After taking Suzanne's workshop, I had a clean slate to work with, and I created the possibility of just connecting with someone. If it led to a relationship, great; if not, great. The important part was I created how I was going to be for myself, for a possible love interest and, most importantly, for my daughter when I was in a relationship. I gave myself a new outlook on love that I could powerfully step into. I'm now in a relationship that has continued to grow and blossom for over two years. I continue to use the techniques I learned in Suzanne's workshop nearly three years ago to grow my relationship and steer it in directions that inspire my boyfriend, my daughter and me. I am truly grateful that I am free to express myself fully in this area of my life."

Remember Virginia, who I met at a bar in Colorado: "Suzanne recommended setting my stage at home with suggestions of romance. A sentimental card of a couple stepping through a puddle huddled under an umbrella is part of my bathroom décor now. One of the homework assignments was to write a Love Letter to myself. I must admit it was satisfying to finally write the words that I longed to hear. The man of my dreams will materialize, and I know he will come to me my way. Suzanne's gentle guidance allowed me to feel safe with being okay alone, but available to the possibilities of flirtation. I do not have a storybook ending to tell here, other than my life is full and satisfying. Because of doing the practices with Suzanne, I am confident with my work and with my relationships. I'm excited to meet the man who is to be my healthy partner when he arrives."

Remember Jill, the high-powered executive: "I ventured back into the dating world with extraordinary results. I trust in my inner and outer beauty, I trust that there are millions of great men in the world who would be honored to call me their own, and I trust that as long as I honor myself and my needs, a healthy relationship is only a matter of time. Case in point, two weeks ago I had four phone calls with men I met online. Two of the calls did not flow. In the past, I would have gone on dates with them anyway, and this time I did not. I boldly told these men during our initial calls that I was not feeling a connection and I wished them well. The two other phone calls were instant connections, so I accepted dates."

Remember Donna, the single mom who is now happily married as a result of trying something new and going country dancing: "In February 2011, I was out dancing when someone asked me to dance. I had no idea that this would be the man of my dreams! At this point, I knew exactly who I was and what I wanted in a partner and in a relationship. I was able just to open up and be with him. It was magical—so much so that we were married six months later! I am truly blessed to have such an amazing man in my life. I know I wouldn't have this if it hadn't been for Suzanne's workshop where I got all that leftover junk out of the way so I could actually SEE him. I will be forever grateful!"

All of these women were in different stages when they started their journeys. You may get disappointed and discouraged from time to time. You may even need a break to regroup. Just remember, YOU can do this! When you come across that amazing man for you, trust that you will know it and will be able to use all of the insights you have gained to be honored, cherished, loved and adored.

For more information please visit www.happylivingforever.com or you can contact me directly at loveable@happylivingforever.com.

Acknowledgements

When people say it takes a village to accomplish something long and challenging, they aren't kidding. Writing this book was not easy for me. I don't consider myself a natural-born writer, yet it was worth every moment. I'm grateful that I listened to my inner voice as it gently pushed and reminded me that I can do it one small step at a time, and not to the voice that wanted to argue.

I want to thank my boyfriend **Stefan Heinz**. Many times I sat in his arms at the kitchen table, crying and wanting to quit. He gently, compassionately and quietly held me tight and let me cry until I was finished. He listened to me, celebrated my successes, and picked me up from the failures. He let me gripe about being insecure about my writing skills, whipped up afternoon cappuccinos, and came up with great ideas. Stefan, I love you with all my heart. You are not just a boyfriend, you are my playmate and teammate. I know you are truly committed that I have a great life. Thank you for growing with me through the stages of adjusting to a new country and writing my first book, and most of all, for allowing me to be me. I love sharing life with you. I can't wait to create more great memories together.

A heartfelt thank you goes to my family: John, Arlene, Teri, Mike, and Kim. Although my family lives far away, their unconditional love for me is always with me. My family has gone through some difficult times. Through it, we are connected at the heart, forever and always. Thank you for loving me and watching me grow over the years. I love you!

My mom, **Arlene Muller,** has herself written a book called *How to Survive and Maybe Even Love Health Professions Schools: Retention and Career Placement Guide*. Thank you, Mom, for your gentle insights, ideas and edits as the book progressed. You were privy to the content during the development phase. It was so much fun to bond with you through writing this book. Thank you for always sprinkling me with your love and, especially, being a pillar of confidence for me.

A warm thank you goes to **Shannon Street, Annemarie Milisen, Alie Olsen, Carrie Franklin and David Brockman** for being my champions and loving and supporting me in every way. They helped me through packing and moving to Switzerland. This included selling my belongings, opening their homes, driving me to the airport, wiping my tears, and sending me off. They even made sure I settled into my new home from afar and felt connected. Those things mean more to me than you will ever know. Your friendship and love are precious, and our connection is deeper than just Denver, Colorado. It's worldwide and wherever we go.

I especially want to thank my **clients** for inspiring me, trusting me, and believing in the work I offer and the difference it makes in their lives. Your courage, openness, vulnerability and strength warms my heart. You all make me a better person every day when you open your hearts and create the relationships of your dreams.

Without the inspiration, expertise and love of **Kristen Moeller**, author of *Waiting for Jack*, this book would not have been possible. As my writing coach and friend, she inspired me every step of the way. When her house burned down in a wildfire and she lost everything, she continued writing. That was the tipping point for me. I figured if she could continue to write and forward her goal after losing her home and all of her belongings, then I could write while moving from the States to Switzerland.

She never gave up on me, even when I dropped out of her book-writing group in 2011. I knew in my heart it wasn't the right time. It was difficult to acknowledge at the time, and I'm glad I listened to my gut. Kristen graciously honored me and let me join a writing group the following year. When I realized the first 45,000 words simply didn't reflect me anymore, Kristen put my mind at ease by showing me that as my life had changed, the book's purpose had transformed as well.

I had streamlined my life down to three suitcases and a laptop, and I was living abroad with my amazing boyfriend. It was perfect to scrap those first words and write a book that reflected who I had become and what I authentically wanted to contribute to women in the world. The writing was a therapeutic exercise to release the past slew of ex-boyfriends, so I consider it time well lived. I was able to focus on the smaller, simpler book I was meant to write.

So, to Kristen I say: Thank you for coaching me through the ups and downs in this journey. Your wisdom was invaluable, encouraging and always from the heart. When I made the decision to move to another continent, I didn't know how that would affect the book. You stayed by my side through it all and kept me focused to the finish line.

A special thank you goes to my writing group: **Gin, Sara, Renata and Kristen** who inspired me with their ups and downs, and listened to me as I went through mine. Thank you for all of your courage and encouragement. It was so nice to have your support in the beginning stages of writing my first book. I am very grateful you gave me that support structure, without which I'm sure this book would not have happened.

Jennifer Coken is special to me. She and I wrote together almost every day for six months. We wrote, edited, scratched our heads, shared feedback and sometimes asked ourselves, "Why are we doing this again?" If it weren't for you and our scheduled time together, I would not have hit my deadline. Thank you for being my consistent writing partner and allowing me to bounce ideas off of you and be vulnerable. I love your book *When I Die, Take My Panties.* The title still makes me grin, and it's a beautiful tribute to your mom. My book actually started when we were roommates, and now the Atlantic Ocean divides us. Yet, we are still, and always will be, connected at the heart level.

My editors are "stars": **Alice Crider, Mary Ann Tate, Sherilyn Dunn** and **Gabbie Shafer**. Although learning to be patient and wait for the manuscript to come back was the most challenging for me, working with each of you has been a pleasure. Trusting your attention to detail and precision actually made the process easier. I have a tendency to be independent. Surrendering to your knowledge and expertise helped me learn that I can accept contribution and constructive criticism and receive your love at the same time. I could not have hit my deadline without you and your brilliant and exceptional talents.

Thank you to **Kimberly Leonard** at Bookcovers.com. I handed you a tight deadline based on my travels to California and Colorado, and you worked closely with me every step of the way. Your commitment that the book cover design and internal formatting be professional and capture the essence of the book, message and author was amazing. You reassured me every step of the way, and you took pride in my book. I appreciated your commitment that I, your customer, am pleased and happy with it, and I love it.

David Lazaroff with **Expressionist Press**, thank you for guiding me through the publishing process and having it be fun. Your knowledge, resources, and dedication to my work allowed me to surrender to the time it takes to produce a book of high quality that honors my readers. You are really a pleasure to work with. You are a conduit for happiness and love, another reason why I'm excited to have you as my partner and publisher. Thank you for being there for me and assisting me in fulfilling a dream come true.

I wish I could thank all of you individually. Please know you've touched my life and have been a contribution to me in a special way, and I have the deepest appreciation for who you are: Clay Collins, Maureen McNamara, Shoshanna French Stokes, Sheila Flanagan, Jennifer Seeley, Melissa Garcia, Barb Tobias, Bert Miranda, Alan Shook, Christie Marie Sheldon, Donna Allgood, Jill Christensen, Angela Casias, Donna Scott, Virginia Clair, David Costantino, Bronagh O'Leary, Jeff Baker, Corrina Sephora Mensoff, Andrea Ray, Jennifer Piehl, Rachel Goren, Sheila Wright, Abbie Weiss, Emma Little, Kim Black-Totham, Jerry Fishman, Sariel Beckenstein, Sue Patterson, Annemarie Leyden, Jeremy Savage, Della Croteau, Ellen Gold, Josh Hirsch, Heather Lockert, Tamarra Oras, Matt Kaplan, Heidi Lelke, Lauren Byrne, Richard Booth, Marie Soderberg, Dede Deane, Cathy Tutty, Jean DiGiovanna, Andrea Floyd, Ann Edwards, Cory Michelle Johnson, Lisa Robinson, Ray Coleman, Rebecca Allanson, Penny Berman, Barry Berman, Stephen Ludwig, Donnie Van Gilder, Genny Lund, Dele Peterson, Rory Esber Dominguez, Marfrisa Geronimo Gipner, Vicki Rosenberg,

Kristyn Kellner, Zanzibar Vermiglio, Raemi Vermiglio, David Cunningham, Jeanine Soloman, Tom Soloman, Jerry Burkhard, Michael Simmons, Kimberly Faye, Amber Witte, Kevin Beltran, Aria Raphael, Birgit Mueller, Shannon Murphy Schmidtke, Trudy Schapansky, Rebecca Jehorek, Robert Skinner, Linda Hampton, David Cotrell, Laurie Kagan, Tony Urbalejo, Oscar Aguirre, Askia Howell, Larry Stanley, Dan Power, Renee Quintana Nunez, Asha Ginda, Sam Peart, Holly Bailey-Peart, Nicolette Vajtey, Sofia Lock, Joy Niederhauser, Christian Callen, Esther Shapiro, Sierra Neblina, Tara Lindis-Corbell, Ann Winton, Linda Selub, Peggy Sue Hauptli Schmoldt, Nora Tomlin, Dani Zerbib, Michelle Zerbib, Laura Kirkham Waggoner, Tim Young, Lane Monson, Jeff Fountain, Barbara Fountain, Dan Raynor, Anne Peterson, Michael Heinz, Tiffany Jones, Anna Fivecoat, Nancy Burton, Helga Christian, Lily Starr, Joani Bisson, Autumn Beamon, Soloman Madron, Tammi DeVille, Laura Squirek, Jeff Jenkins, Rob Maxwell, Alan Bryner, Joseph Dimasi, Gail Lacroix, Eric Princen, Omak Yanez, Dean Schaner, Dawn Marsh, Dale Kershner, Lynn Ellis, John Osborn, Jeff Jenkins, Marcie Young, Jeff Belanger, Taryn Schroeder, Marion Harwood, Brie Monroe, Scott Weeden, etc.

CPSIA information can be obtained
at www.ICGtesting.com
Printed in the USA
BVHW03s0602110818
523996BV00003B/7/P

9 780985 163143